Dancing with the Devil

Dancing with the Devil

Why Bad Feelings Make Life Good

KRISTA K. THOMASON

OXFORD
UNIVERSITY PRESS

OXFORD
UNIVERSITY PRESS

Oxford University Press is a department of the University of Oxford. It furthers
the University's objective of excellence in research, scholarship, and education
by publishing worldwide. Oxford is a registered trade mark of Oxford University
Press in the UK and certain other countries.

Published in the United States of America by Oxford University Press
198 Madison Avenue, New York, NY 10016, United States of America.

Library of Congress Cataloging-in-Publication Data
Names: Thomason, Krista K., author.
Title: Dancing with the devil : why bad feelings make life good / Krista K. Thomason.
Description: New York : Oxford University Press, [2024] |
Includes bibliographical references and index.
Identifiers: LCCN 2023013841 (print) | LCCN 2023013842 (ebook) |
ISBN 9780197673287 (hb) | ISBN 9780197673300 (epub)
Subjects: LCSH: Emotions. | Negativity (Philosophy) | Well-being. |
Emotions.
Classification: LCC BF531 .T53 2024 (print) | LCC BF531 (ebook) |
DDC 152.4—dc23/eng/20230624
LC record available at https://lccn.loc.gov/2023013841
LC ebook record available at https://lccn.loc.gov/2023013842

DOI: 10.1093/oso/9780197673287.001.0001

Printed by Sheridan Books, Inc., United States of America

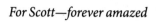

For Scott—forever amazed

Contents

Acknowledgments

I've spent most of my life being told to calm down. My feelings have always been too big and too loud, in need of what sometimes feels like constant correction. If I'm angry, I should relax. If I'm sad, I should cheer up. If I complain, I should look on the bright side. It's not an accident that I've spent the majority of my career writing about emotions and defending the ones nobody likes. This book is partly for my younger self who didn't know how to value her emotions and for those, like her, who never seem to feel the right things.

Many thanks are due forever to my mentors: David Sussman, Helga Varden, and Terrence McConnell. Their influence in my life is what allowed me to gather the courage to be a philosopher in the first place.

There are many philosophers of emotion to whom I owe a deep debt of intellectual gratitude, but I want to make special mention of Jeffrie Murphy, who died in 2020. Reading his work while I was in graduate school was an awakening. We corresponded over email, and he was incredibly kind to me as a young scholar. I never got the chance to meet him or to tell him to his face how much his work meant to me. Let this be a lesson to us all: don't be stingy with your appreciation. I offer this book as a tribute to his memory and as thanks for showing me what philosophical work on emotions could be.

The National Humanities Center (NHC) is a humanist's paradise, and I was able to complete nearly all of my book because of my in-residence fellowship there. I was the Philip L. Quinn fellow during the 2021–2022 academic year. Thank you to Robert

Newman, Matthew Booker, Lynn Miller, Karen Mudd, Stephanie Tucker, Brooke Andrade, Joe Milillo, Sarah Harris, Joel Elliott, and the rest of the truly marvelous staff for their amazing support. My wonderful peers, Mavis Biss, Laura Papish, Karen Stohr, and Zach Hoskins, were kind enough to write letters of support for my NHC application, so thank you to them for believing in the project. Thank you to Michelle Crouch, the Assistant Director of Sponsored Programs at Swarthmore, who read multiple drafts of my application materials and made them so much better. Thanks also to all of the fellows in my cohort who talked with me about the ideas in the book and listened to me voice never-ending doubts about what I was doing. The NHC is a place where you can feel the passion for the humanities in the very bones of the building. It's a place where humanist scholarship can genuinely flourish, and I am grateful that it exists.

Thank you to my home institution, Swarthmore College, for extra financial resources that allowed me to go to the National Humanities Center. Thanks also to my wonderful colleagues in the Philosophy Department for their continuing support. My students at Swarthmore may not see themselves directly in these pages, but they should know that they were part of the audience that I was imagining as I was writing. Thank you to my incredible editor, Lucy Randall, for her thoughtful feedback on the manuscript and for believing in the book. Thanks also to Rachel Perkins, who designed the perfect cover. I am grateful to everyone at Oxford University Press for making the dream a reality. Thank you to Cara Anderson and Alisa Giardinelli in the Communications Office at Swarthmore for helping me with book promotion.

I presented portions of my book in several venues, and the feedback I received from those audiences helped me refine my ideas. Thanks to the Contempt and Public Life Workshop participants (especially to Zach Hoskins and Joan Woolfrey for organizing), the University of Nottingham Philosophy Department, and the Parr Center for Ethics at the University of North Carolina, Chapel Hill.

I listen to music while I write, and I want to thank the musicians that comprise my many playlists. There are too many to name, but a very special mention is due to the heavy metal bands because they are my nearest and dearest: Judas Priest, Iron Maiden, Dio, Black Sabbath, Mastodon, and Motörhead.

Some of the most important people in a scholar's life are the ones who are willing to read your messy first drafts and help you talk through early ideas. Thank you to my beautiful friends: Glen Baity, Ashely Lefrak Grider, Logan Grider, Zach Hoskins, and Gregory Pappas. Your graduate school friends are some of the best you'll ever have, and a special thanks is due to Aaron Harper and Brandon Polite for reading lots of drafts and for putting up with me all these years.

Last but not least, the people who have been with me the longest. Mom, Dad, and Kerry: thank you for all the years of love and support. Without you, I wouldn't be here. Shelly and Sarah: you are my oldest and dearest friends, and I'm grateful every day for you. And Scott, who is my favorite reader, the love of my life, the center of my world, and the best thing to ever happen to me: no words would ever be enough. My eyes have always followed you around the room. They always will.

PART I

THE GARDEN

"A wild, where weeds and flow'rs promiscuous shoot;
Or garden, tempting with forbidden fruit"

Alexander Pope, *Essay on Man*

"Philosophy is not a making of a home for the mind out of
reality.

It is more like learning to leave things be: restoration in
the wilderness, here and now"

Henry Bugbee, *The Inward Morning*

Introduction

Weeds, Worms, and Communing with the Dead

Imagine you have a garden. It's lush and green with beautiful flowers, and like all gardens it requires tending. You go out dutifully to do the necessary work, but every day, there they are: the weeds. You try to get rid of them, but they never seem to stay gone for good. Sometimes you successfully pull them up, but new ones always appear in their place. In the hot, sticky stretches of summer, you might go a few days without tending. When you go back outside, the weeds have gotten worse. That's what weeds do: they take over and spoil gardens.

This garden is your life and bad feelings—feelings like anger, envy, spite, and contempt—are the weeds. They need to be pulled up before they choke out the nice plants. You may not be able to get rid of them completely, but you're supposed to battle them as best you can. Maybe you try to keep them small and manageable, or maybe you douse them with the strongest weed killer you can buy. No matter what strategy you use, your relationship to the weeds is always the same. Weeds are things to get rid of or control. The best garden is one with no weeds, and the best life is one with no bad feelings.

We need to change this way of thinking. Bad feelings are the worms, not the weeds. They're just below the surface, and if you dig around even a little bit, you'll see them—slimy and crawly, churning in the dirt. Worms make most people squeamish. Many of us would rather just admire the flowers and forget the worms are there. But that would be a mistake. Worms are as much a part of the garden as the flowers, and their presence means your garden is thriving. Wishing away your worms is wishing away the richness and texture of the garden itself. So, if you want to keep your garden as lovely as it is, you had better figure out how to embrace the wriggly inhabitants. This book will help you love your worms.

If I want to convince you that bad feelings are good, I need to offer an apology for them. This isn't the kind of apology where you say, "I'm sorry." A less familiar kind of apology has its roots in the Greek word *apologia*, which means a speech in defense of something. Philosophers know the second definition well because of Plato. An ancient Greek from Athens, Plato lived from about 429 to 347 BC during a time of political upheaval. The ugly aftermath of war and power struggles in Athens unfortunately ensnared his beloved teacher and friend, Socrates. In Plato's dialogue, the *Apology*, Socrates appears before the Athenian court on charges of impiety and corruption of the youth. While the jurors might have been expecting a speech from Socrates that resembled "I'm sorry," they got something that looked a lot more like "Let me explain why I am right." Socrates' apology was not received kindly, and he was sentenced to death. Given the track record, you would think philosophers would be wary of these kinds of apologies, but it hasn't seemed to deter us.

Negative emotions, both inside and outside philosophy, are widely seen as obstacles to a good life. Since bad feelings prevent us from living well, so this reasoning goes, we need to do something with them. Some people argue that we have to do our best to not feel them. Others argue that we just need to feel them in the "right way" or to "channel" them into something good. If we are really going to value bad feelings, we need to reject the first premise of the argument: bad feelings are not obstacles to a good life. They have a bad reputation that they don't really deserve and our suspicion of them comes from mistaken ideas about what human emotional life is supposed to look like. Just like worms are part of a garden, bad feelings are part of a good life.

Before we get ahead of ourselves, what exactly are we talking about when we talk about bad feelings? "Feelings" is a broad term. We apply it to everything from the love parents have for their children to the pins-and-needles sensation we get when our arms fall asleep. There are interesting things to say about all these, but we will be focusing on the feelings that we usually call emotions.

Living with Our Emotions

Philosophers have been thinking about emotions since they started thinking, which means they've developed many theories about them.[1] Theories can clarify and organize our thinking about emotions, which is helpful. But a theory that tells you what an emotion is may not help you figure out how to live well with your emotions. This is the question we'll be examining: how do bad feelings fit into a good life? We can call this the "practical problem" that emotions pose. It isn't a problem in a negative sense. A problem is just something we have to figure out (like a math problem). A practical problem is a problem about how to live.

To see what the practical problem looks like, let's start with a story of an emotional experience. The 19th-century philosopher Anna Julia Cooper was born into slavery in North Carolina. Once slavery was abolished, she was able to get an education, earning a BA, a master's in mathematics, and eventually a PhD. Her best-known work is *A Voice from the South* (1892), which is a collection of essays on a broad range of topics, including the importance of education and the difficulties facing Black women in America. In one of the essays, Cooper describes an experience common for Black women traveling alone by train. She explains how conductors help White women step off the train onto the platform by taking their arms or holding their luggage. When Black women get off the train, the conductors "deliberately fold their arms and turn around" in a clear refusal to help.[2] Cooper then describes how this treatment makes her feel. She calls it the feeling of "slighted womanhood:"

> It's poignancy, compared with which Juno's *spretae injuria formae* [insult to her spurned beauty] is earthly and vulgar, is holier than that of jealousy, deeper than indignation, tenderer than rage. Its first impulse of wrathful protest and proud self-vindication is checked and shamed by the consciousness that self-assertion would outrage still further the same delicate instinct.[3]

Cooper writes in beautiful 19th-century style and eloquently narrates her emotional experience with classical allusions and poetic language. We've lost the knack for describing our feelings with such flair. She starts with an allusion to an ancient Greek myth called the Judgment of Paris: a beauty contest between Juno (queen of the gods), Venus, and Minerva. It was judged by Paris, a mortal who was known for his fairness (although not so much for his foresight). Paris gives the prize (a golden apple) to Venus, so naturally Juno feels insulted—especially since her divine beauty is judged by a mere mortal. Cooper describes her own feeling as *worse* than even Juno's outrage.

Yet she also describes it in delicate and complimentary terms, such as "holy" and "tender." This suggests that she doesn't think of her anger as purely negative. We might say she thinks her anger is warranted: she has every right to be insulted. She knows all too well that the train conductors are treating her unfairly because of her race. But Cooper's emotions are also at odds with each other. While she feels justified in her anger, she's also ashamed of it. She's afraid it confirms the very thing the train conductor thinks: that she's not really a proper lady after all. Even though she has every right to be angry, the strength of her outrage catches her off-guard and she's not sure what to do with it. While we may not describe our feelings the way a 19th-century philosopher would, we've likely had complex emotional experiences like this.

Cooper's description helps us get a clearer picture of what emotions are and what they do. Emotions are sort of like a sixth sense—they tell you things about the world.[4] Your five senses can tell you that you're on a walk in the woods. You see the trees, hear the birds, and smell the earthiness of the fallen leaves. Your emotions tell you how the walk feels—that it's serene, lonely, or creepy. Emotions tell us things about what's happening around us, about our relations with other people, and about our own sense of who we are. Cooper's anger tells her that the train conductor turning his back on her is an insult. Her anger also tells her how she sees herself—a woman who deserves to be treated with the same respect that White women get from train conductors.

Sometimes our emotions realize things before we do.[5] If you feel frustrated and angry at work every day, it's probably a sign that something isn't right. If you feel nervous and giddy in the presence of another person, you might have romantic feelings for them. If hanging out with your friend makes you miserable, that person might not be your friend after all. Sometimes our emotions help us discover things about ourselves that we're surprised to learn. You hop on a roller coaster expecting to have a good time, but it turns out you're white-knuckle terrified during the entire ride. Like our other senses, the information we get from our emotions may not always match what's happening in the world. If you've ever wondered whether you're overreacting to a coworker's comment, you're asking whether or not your emotions are perceiving the situation the right way. You can see this in Cooper's experience, too. She's angry at the train conductor, but she's also conflicted about how angry she has a right to be.

Emotions are also reflections of what we care about or what matters to us. In a different book, I've argued that emotions are *constitutive* of our commitments and the things we value.[6] To use myself as an example, philosophy is one of my commitments—I've devoted my life to it and it matters to me. Because I care about it, I'm susceptible to a whole set of emotions about it. I feel joy when I get to read a philosophy book, I feel anger when people say bad things about philosophy, and I feel disappointed when my students don't like the texts I assign in class. I wouldn't feel joy, anger, or disappointment if I didn't care. Being recognized as a proper lady mattered a lot to Cooper. She was a woman of distinction: she could read at least four languages, earned multiple college degrees, was a dedicated educator, and an advocate for social change. Not only did she feel that she had earned respect because of her accomplishments, it was just blatant discrimination that she was treated differently from White women. When train conductors refused to give her the respect and courtesy she deserved, she couldn't be indifferent to it. She was angry, ashamed, and wounded because she cared. If she felt none of these things—if the insult simply rolled off of her—we'd assume that being treated with respect didn't matter to her. Feeling about something is a way of caring about it.

Our emotions are an important part of our lives, but that doesn't mean our relationship to them is always easy. To begin with, our emotions can be more and less clear to us. If I pull back the shower curtain and there's a snake in my tub, there's no doubt I'm afraid, but many cases aren't like this. Sometimes we struggle to identify our emotions—am I angry or am I just frustrated? We also struggle to articulate them—I know I feel *something*, but I don't know what it is. It can be hard to explain your feelings. I might be sad and yet have no idea why. Our feelings can also surprise us. You might find yourself caught off-guard by your jealousy toward your spouse's new coworker. Someone's harsh comment hurts me more than I expected, and I suddenly find tears in my eyes.

Our feelings can surprise or confuse us because they are partly under our control and partly not under our control. We don't always feel the ones we want to feel or expect to feel. We can't force ourselves to feel something we don't, and we can't always "turn off" our feelings no matter how much we'd like to. At the same time, we have some kind of influence over them. I can calm myself down if I don't want to be angry. I can cheer myself up when I'm sad. I can learn to let go of my guilt. If our emotions were automatic like reflexes or digestion, there wouldn't be much we could do about them. If our emotions were fully under our control, we could select them much like we pick out a shirt from the closet. The trouble is that emotions are somewhere in between, and it's not clear where on the spectrum they are.

On top of all this, we evaluate or judge our emotions—we feel things about our feelings. This is partly what is happening with Cooper: she is both angry and at the same time partly ashamed of her anger. You can (as the singer Joan Jett would say) hate yourself for loving someone. You might be frustrated with yourself when a family member lays an unfair guilt trip on you and it works. Sometimes we judge ourselves too harshly for our emotions, especially when they might be trying to tell us something valuable and important. Sometimes we don't judge ourselves harshly enough: we use our emotions as excuses when we act irresponsibly. We can feel too much and we can feel too little, and we criticize ourselves for both.

Since emotions are part of us, but they also have a life of their own, we have to figure out how to live with them. That's what makes them a practical problem, and that's what we'll tackle together in this book. Before we begin, I want to dispel some common myths about emotions. Let me start with what I call "head versus heart."

Head versus Heart

The idea of the head versus heart is old, but most people associate it with Romanticism. Romanticism was an intellectual and cultural movement that had its peak in Europe toward the end of the 1800s.[7] Romantics loved emotional melodrama. Yearning unrequited love, stormy inner turmoil, and the sweet pangs of melancholy— these are all popular Romantic themes. Their love of this melodrama was a product of their philosophical ideas. For many of the

Romantics, our natural feelings and sympathies were good guides to living well, if you were careful to listen to them and kept them free from corruption. Corruption came in several forms. The poet William Wordsworth named urban life, extravagance, and spending too much time courting vapid high society as corrupting forces.[8] Another form of corruption was the worship of the power of reason. The Romantics were particularly critical of what they saw as a stifling education that they associated with universities. Too much emphasis on formal knowledge obscures and distorts our ability to, as Wordsworth puts it, look at the world "in a spirit of love."[9] Being too rational can deaden your feelings.

There's a little piece of the Romantics in our contemporary idea of the head versus the heart.[10] It assumes that reason and emotion are different or separate and that they are usually in conflict with each other. You sometimes hear people say things like, "My head says one thing, but my heart says another" or "Think about this logically. You're letting your emotions get in the way." Your head and your heart pull you in different directions.

But the contrast between reason and emotion isn't so stark. Reasoning isn't emotionless. When we think that reason is devoid of feeling, we're assuming that all reason is "objective" reason.[11] Objective reason is harder to define than you might think, but the stereotypical image of it is found in 1960s TV shows. Joe Friday, one of the detectives from *Dragnet*, was famous for saying things like, "All we want are the facts, ma'am."[12] Half-human and half-Vulcan, Mr. Spock from the original *Star Trek* was portrayed as having no strong emotions. He frequently observed that his human shipmates like Captain Kirk and Dr. McCoy, were "most illogical." Objective reason, so these images tell us, is all about getting the facts right— no opining, no poetics, and no feelings. How we feel doesn't change the cold, hard facts.

The problem with this image is that it assumes that reason's only job is to determine the facts. Think about any big decision you've made in your life: moving to a new place, switching careers, or starting a family. Lots of reasoning goes into these decisions. Of course, you need facts to make your choice (how much is my new salary and is it enough to live comfortably?), but the facts all by themselves won't give you the answer. We often have to appeal to the things we care about or the things that matter to us in order to determine which facts are the most relevant. If I thrive in the energy of a big city, all the money in the world wouldn't draw me to a job opportunity in a rural place. This isn't emotion conquering reason or reason conquering emotion. Deliberating about your life doesn't fit neatly into either the reason box or the emotion box.

Not only does reason involve emotions, emotions involve reason. Head versus heart sometimes assumes that emotions are more like reflexes, much like your pupils dilate when you enter a dark room.[13] Philosophers have pointed out that emotions operate with their own logic. We sometimes describe this as the "aboutness" of emotions. Aboutness is built into the way we talk about our emotions. We say things like, "I'm angry *about* this meeting" or "I'm sad *about* the movie." Since emotions are about things, we can give reasons why we feel them. If I run into an axe murderer in the woods, I'm afraid. Philosophers will argue that my fear is the right or appropriate response to my circumstances: after all, I'm in danger. The person who feels fear in the face of real danger is having a rational response.

Our feelings are also responsive to new reasons and to new information in a way that reflexes aren't. If someone tells me that the axe murderer is actually just a realistic-looking plywood cutout for my neighbor's haunted house, my fear will eventually go away (it might take me some time to calm down, of course). Also, if emotions were like reflexes, there would be no difference between rational and irrational feelings. Yet we make this distinction all the time. It's not rational to refuse to leave your house because you *might* come across an axe murderer, especially if you have no evidence that there is one outside. The fact that some fears are irrational doesn't make fear itself irrational.

Questions about the rationality of our emotions will come up again later because people often think that negative emotions are always irrational. For now, we should leave head versus heart behind. It's not always clear where the head ends and the heart takes over. Heads and hearts live together in the same person.

Students of Nature

Another common idea that people have about emotions is that they're all in the brain. We often assume that psychology, biology, or neuroscience are the fields to turn to if we want to learn about emotions—we should study them scientifically. It might sound cutting-edge, but this way of thinking emotions dates back at least to Aristotle, one of Plato's students who lived in the 4th century BC.

In one of his best-known works, *De Anima* ("On the Soul"), Aristotle explains that we can think about emotions either as "a student of nature" or "a student of dialectic." While the student of dialectic will define anger, for example, as "an appetite for giving pain in return," the student of nature will define it as "a boiling of the blood around the heart."[14] The first definition appeals to reasons why people typically get angry, while the second focuses on the biological or physiological causes of anger.

The student of nature studies emotions in the same way you would study other natural objects, like the shell of an oyster or nitrogen in the atmosphere. The neuroscientist Antonio Damasio provides a contemporary example. According to Damasio, all living organisms (humans included) are governed by "automated homeostatic regulation," which is the collection of all the biological systems that help keep us alive—everything from our metabolism to our immune systems.[15] Our emotions are products of this collection of systems, and they also contribute to homeostasis. Fear, for example, is a neurobiological response that has evolved to help us get out of dangerous situations. Emotions both help individual organisms survive and promote pro-social behavior that contributes to the survival of the species as a whole.

There's nothing wrong with this picture, so far as it goes.[16] Unfortunately, when people start giving student-of-nature explanations, you often hear something like the following: "Emotions are *just* chemical reactions in the brain" or "Emotions are *really* survival mechanisms." The little words "just" and "really" are punching above their weight. People who talk this way imply that all there is to know about emotions can be discovered by the student of nature. As this reasoning goes, understanding the biological or neurological processes behind our emotions tells us the real story about them.

But what do we mean by "the real story?" The 19th-century American philosopher William James gives a colorful example. He writes, "A Beethoven string quartet is truly . . . a scraping of horses' tails on cats' bowels."[17] The "scraping of horses' tails on cats' bowels" is a reference to the material that the bows and strings are made of: violin bows are made of horsehair, and the strings are made from catgut (not actually derived from cats; it's from the intestines of livestock animals). So, is a Beethoven string quartet "truly" the scraping of horse tails on cat's bowels? It is if you think the only way to "truly" describe something is to identify its material causes or explain its underlying mechanics. But think about all the ways we can describe a Beethoven string quartet. We can investigate the history of Beethoven's arranging of the quartet. We can discuss the relations of the movements to each other as well as the overall musical structure of the piece. We can say that his string quartets mix sprightly elements with dramatic undertones. These are all ways to understand a string quartet. Why is the catgut story the real one and these aren't?

The catgut story is what philosophers call *reductive*. Reductive explanations try to reduce (hence the name) a complex phenomenon into a simpler one or into simpler parts. People often assume that simple explanations are always the best explanations.

Sometimes they are helpful, but sometimes they aren't. It depends on what exactly you want to understand. If someone is trying to understand the differences between Beethoven's string quartet and Dvořák's, telling them that a string quartet is *really* horsehair on catgut is no answer at all.

The same is true for emotions. Knowing that emotions are the result of biological, neurological, or evolutionary processes doesn't answer the question: how do we live well with our emotions? Think back to Cooper's experience of slighted womanhood. Were you to tell Cooper that her alternating and conflicting anger, shame, and pain are part of her homeostasis regulation, what would this mean to her? How would this help her negotiate her feelings? Should she simply tell herself that her emotions are neurobiological processes? And then what? The story that the student of nature tells isn't necessarily meant to be practical advice. Of course, it could function that way—maybe if we think of emotions as part of the natural order of things, it will help us live with them. But how? There's no automatic answer to the practical problem of emotions that simply falls out once we gather all the natural facts about them. There is still philosophy to do.

Students of Dialectic

In this book, we will be looking at emotions from the other perspective that Aristotle gives us: the student of dialectic. The term *dialectic* in philosophy has a wide range of meanings. For our purposes, dialectic means investigating a topic through questioning and conversation with others. Part of that process is collecting what Aristotle calls *endoxa*, or opinions from people who have thought about the topic you're interested in.[18] We collect *endoxa* because the student of dialectic thinks about emotions as people experience them from the first-person perspective. Return to Aristotle's example of anger: the student of dialectic says it's "the appetite for giving pain in return." You don't have to agree with this definition, but you can see how it works. It identifies anger by what we typically do with it or by what anger is about. It's the sort of definition we would come up with if we gathered together people who have felt anger before and asked them to pick out its defining characteristics.

Once you collect *endoxa* and get an idea of what anger is, the student of dialectic then tests the idea through conversation and questioning. Is anger really an appetite for giving pain in return? What does it mean to say anger is an appetite? What is "pain" in this definition? Does an angry person *always* give pain in return or only sometimes? Can we think of other ways of defining anger and compare them to this one? This may sound abstract, but chances are you've done this yourself. Maybe some incident at work bothers you and you're not sure whether you're overreacting, so you talk to a friend about it. Maybe a family member is mad about something that you think is no big deal, so you listen to them explain why they're angry. When you reflect on your feelings and try to clarify what you feel, you're engaging in emotional dialectic.

Dialectic about emotions is what we'll be doing together in this book. I'll be using my training and skills as a philosopher to unravel the knot we've tied around our bad feelings. I'll draw from a number of different sources: philosophy, fiction, memoirs, and everyday life. This process of gathering sources and sorting through them is the collecting of *endoxa*. And it will require us to commune with the dead.

I Read Dead People

For my husband's fortieth birthday, we took a trip to New Orleans. While we were browsing a used bookstore (this is how a philosopher and a fiction writer do vacations), I found a book of poetry by one of my favorite poets, e.e. cummings. I leafed through the pages, debating whether to buy it, and suddenly a sticker fell out onto the floor. It had a black background with white letters that read "I Read Dead People." I bought the book.

I'm a humanist who is trained in the history of philosophy, so communing with the dead is what I do. Reading dead people is collecting *endoxa*. You might wonder why we should gather the opinions of the dead—why not stick to the latest work on emotions? The 20th-century English philosopher Bertrand Russell described a certain danger we sometimes fall into. He called it being "parochial in time." Being parochial in time is a way of being narrowminded and overconfident. Russell explained that people who are parochial in time "feel a contempt for the past that it does not deserve, and for the present a respect it deserves still less."[19]

If we don't want to be parochial in time, we have to get over our contempt for the past. People from the past are a lot like us. Every new generation of humans faces big questions about their existence. Many of those questions are the same ones that have faced all human beings from the moment we were able to ask them. How should I live? What should I believe? What is the meaning of my life? For those of us who happen to be born in the present day, there is no sense in reinventing the wheel as we try to make our way through these tough questions. Reading what dead people think can give us a head start on our own answers.

Those of us living in the present often mistakenly think that we know better than dead people do. Their world was ignorant and we've made progress since then. We have penicillin and they had leeches. We usually fail to realize that future generations will see our penicillin as leeches. We judge dead people harshly at our own peril: the future will be as unkind to us as we are to them. Once we get over our prejudice toward the past, we realize that our assumptions about it are often false. Dig a little deeper and it turns out dead people knew what they were talking about. Leeches sound weird, but they weren't a bad idea after all: in 2004, the Food and Drug Administration approved the use of leeches to help restore blood flow after surgery.[20]

We also need to have a little less respect for the present. Dead people can help us here too, but instead of focusing on our similarities, it helps to see our differences. People in the past looked through eyes very much like ours, but they looked at very different worlds. It usually takes experiences with other people, times, and places for us to realize that what seems obvious to us isn't so obvious. Travel to another country and you'll realize the way life is back home is *a* way to live, but not necessarily *the* way. Read a history book and you'll see that our current ideas about anything from gender to property are simply one set of ideas among many. Of course, we should avoid lionizing the past: not everything old is good. But not everything new is better than what came before.

Dead people sometimes know us better than we know ourselves. You read a book and you come across a passage that hits you like a bolt of lightning. It articulates a feeling or a thought that you've had, but you couldn't quite put your finger on. It identifies a problem that you had been unable to see. It feels like this person from the past can see into your very soul. As the writer James Baldwin put it, "You think your pain and your heartbreak are unprecedented in the world and then you read. It was Dostoyevsky and Dickens who taught me that the things that tormented me most were the very things that connected me with all the people who were alive, or who ever had been alive."[21] The distance between you and the past evaporates, and a fellow human soul emerges as a friend.

Montaigne's Flower-Strewn Plateau

You might be wondering: why philosophy? What can philosophers do to help you with your negative emotions? Isn't that a job for a therapist? There are many philosophers, old and new, who think of philosophy as a kind of therapy, but not in the clinical sense that we use today. One of them was the French philosopher Michel de

Montaigne, whose vision of philosophy is the one I'll adopt for this book.

Montaigne was born in 1533 and lived during the Renaissance.[22] When Montaigne's father died, he inherited the family estate and, according to his telling, had planned to retire from all official business to pursue learning. He set up a library in one of the towers of his château. On the wooden beams in the ceiling, he had inscribed various sayings from some of his favorite authors. Montaigne loved ancient Greek and Roman philosophers—so much so that he could even quote some of them from memory. Learned life wasn't the escape that Montaigne hoped it would be: owning a château was more work than he thought, and his political duties frequently got in the way of his studies. Depressed and anxious, he decided to start writing down his thoughts to get them out of his head. This collection of thoughts eventually became his most famous work, known simply as the *Essays*, first published in 1580. It is a collection of essays of varying lengths on a wide array of topics—everything from cannibals to education to thumbs.

The *Essays* can be a frustrating read for people who are expecting something organized. Montaigne switches between topics without concern for whether they are related. He is also notorious for not reaching any conclusions. Many of the essays simply end, and you find yourself wondering what the point was. Some of this is intentional: Montaigne preferred not to be too settled in his views. He even had his own medal made and engraved with the Greek word *epecho*, which means "I abstain." Montaigne isn't sure of many things, but one thing he is sure of is that philosophy's true aim is to help us live well. He was disgusted by people who thought philosophy was all strife and seriousness: "Whoever clapped that wan and frightening mask on her face!"[23] On the contrary, Montaigne thought philosophy was "fair, triumphant, loving, as delightful as she is courageous." Rather than being "perched on the summit of a steep mountain, rough and inaccessible," she "dwells on a beautiful plateau, fertile and strewn with flowers."[24]

Like the ancient philosophers he loved, Montaigne thought that the proper subject matter of philosophy was human life in all its variations and complexities. He took seriously the ancient edict inscribed at the Oracle of Delphi: "Know thyself." Montaigne interpreted the edict to mean that self-understanding was the key to living well, and he thought philosophy was supposed to help us gain that self-understanding. Sometimes people mistake self-understanding for self-help. The self-help industry usually tries to offer you an easy answer—a one-size-fits all, prepackaged nugget of something that sounds like wisdom. That's not what Montaigne is selling. People don't fit into formulas. We have to learn how to be comfortable with our own complexity, and Montaigne is a master at showing us how to do this. For Montaigne, self-understanding is about exploring your inner wilderness, not pruning yourself into a topiary.

Reading the *Essays* is to walk with Montaigne on his journey through his own mental wilderness. He invites you along as he tries to make sense of himself, his experiences, and his world. In the opening note to the reader, Montaigne writes: "I have not been concerned to serve you nor my reputation." Instead of presenting himself in his best or most flattering light, he says he wants to "be seen in my simple, natural, everyday fashion, without striving or artifice" complete with all his "defects." If he could escape from the demands of social convention, Montaigne assures us that he would have presented himself "whole, and wholly naked."[25] Montaigne isn't coy or shy. He shows you all the parts himself—the flattering, the awkward, and the amusing. He faces himself honestly without tearing himself down or puffing himself up. Montaigne shows his readers how you can accept the weird and ugly parts of yourself without thinking that they spoil everything that is good about you. Coming face-to-face with our negative emotions requires this same gentle honesty. We need to see them for what they really are without wanting to tear them down or puff them up. In facing the worms in your garden with gentle honesty, I hope you decide you want them to stay.

This book is for anyone who wants to think about how to live with their bad feelings. No philosophical expertise is required. I hope the philosophers who are reading will enjoy it, but they need to know that this book is not a scholarly debate. I'll mostly avoid weighing in on the esoteric controversies. Instead, I'll use some of the end notes to mark where the controversies are. I'll begin those notes with "Philosopher's note." Nonphilosophers are perfectly welcome to read them, but you can also skip them if you'd like.

If you want a closer look at the worms in your garden, you are cordially invited to join me and Montaigne on the plateau among the flowers.

1

Emotional Saints

"Saints," George Orwell writes, "should always be judged guilty until they are proved innocent."[1] It's a bold opening line for an essay about the life of Mahātmā Gandhi, especially since it was published only a year after Gandhi was assassinated. It might even sound offensive—this is Gandhi we're talking about. He's on the "who's who" list of inspirational figures. Gandhi was a leader in the fight for India's independence from Orwell's home country of England. He put himself in harm's way for a higher cause and became an inspiration to peaceful movements all over the world. Who does Orwell think he is, being suspicious of a saint?

As the essay unfolds, you realize that Gandhi is Orwell's subject but not his target. The real target is sainthood. Orwell objects to the whole enterprise of sainthood—Gandhi's version and other versions as well. In the essay, Orwell focuses on Gandhi's extremely disciplined lifestyle. Here are some of Gandhi's restrictions: a strict vegetarian diet with no spices or condiments; no alcohol, tea, or tobacco; no luxuries and few domestic comforts; abstention from sex and, if possible, from sexual desire itself; no close friendships or exclusive loving relationships. Gandhi required his family and all of his followers to adhere to the same discipline. His devotion to enlightenment and peace work often caused conflicts with his family. The most serious one was with his oldest son, Harilal.

Harilal joined Gandhi's nonviolence campaign, and it got him imprisoned six times over the course of three years. When he left prison the last time, he decided to give up Gandhi's austere lifestyle. In a series of letters and long conversations, Harilal expressed anger toward his father for his hard-heartedness toward the family and for not thinking about his children's future. Harilal wanted a normal life—an education, a career, and a family. As the oldest son, he thought he was entitled to special consideration from his father.[2] Harilal felt that he played second fiddle to Gandhi's peace work and spiritual enlightenment. Gandhi saw all of the things that Harilal valued as either unnecessary or as obstacles to a higher purpose. Gandhi referred to life without his disciplined commitments as "insipid and animal-like."[3]

Should we fault Harilal for wanting a normal human life instead of wanting a life of disciplined sacrifice? Most people probably wouldn't blame him for making different choices than those of his father. Not everyone is cut out to be a saint. Spiritual enlightenment requires serious sacrifices, and it's an incredible accomplishment. People like Gandhi are just more capable or stronger than the rest of us. Think of all the good that Gandhi did in the world and all the people he inspired. Most of us don't even come close to what he accomplished and that's a shame. Even if we're more like Harilal, we can still admire Gandhi and see him as a role model. Wouldn't the world be a better place if we all tried to be just a little bit more like Gandhi, even if we can't manage to be as enlightened as he was?

Here is where Orwell disagrees. He thinks our admiration of Gandhi is based on a false assumption, namely, that "a human being is a failed saint."[4] The reasoning goes like this: sainthood is the best version of a human life. We would all be better off as saints, but sainthood is difficult and human beings are flawed and lazy, so few people achieve it. Still, we should try our best to get there—the closer to sainthood, the better. But, Orwell asks, *why* should we assume that sainthood is the best version of a human life? Maybe it's not actually that admirable. He writes:

> The essence of being human is that one does not seek perfection, that one *is* sometimes willing to commit sins for the sake of loyalty, that one does not push asceticism to the point where it makes friendly intercourse impossible, and that one is prepared

in the end to be defeated and broken up by life, which is the inevitable price of fastening one's love upon other human individuals.[5]

Orwell's point is that sainthood requires us to try to be less human, but being less human means giving up something valuable. He's not simply saying that we should let a thousand flowers bloom and everyone can decide how to live their own lives. He is arguing that Harilal is right and Gandhi is wrong. Harilal has the right priorities and Gandhi's are out of order. Harilal hasn't failed to live up to his father's high standards. He just wants to be a good human. Being a good human, according to Orwell, is *better* than being a saint. Human beings aren't failed saints. Saints are failed human beings.

Orwell is pressing us to ask the question: what is a good life?[6] Sometimes a good life means a *morally good* life: a life devoted to making the world a better place, helping as many people as possible, saving the planet, having an exemplary character, or achieving the highest form of spiritual enlightenment. Sometimes a good life means a *meaningful* life: a life that's worth living for the person living it. For some people, the morally good life is their version of a meaningful life—people like Mother Teresa or Gandhi find meaning in helping the poor or becoming enlightened. These are Orwell's saints. Other people, like Harilal, find meaning in things that aren't helping the poor or saving the planet. That doesn't mean they're doing anything morally bad: they're not hurting anyone or making the world a worse place. They just find their meaning in regular human vocations, like devoting themselves to their families, creating music, or studying philosophy. Orwell thinks we're tempted to say that finding meaning in the morally good life is the best scenario. People who find meaning in music or philosophy might not be doing anything wrong, but they aren't living the best kind of life they could live. It would be better, so this reasoning goes, if they were Mother Teresa or Gandhi—their lives fall short by comparison.

This is the conclusion that Orwell wants to resist. He argues that there is something *defective* about the saint's life. In order to be a saint, Orwell thinks we have to stop caring or care much less about regular human life. When you're on a mission to save the world or achieve spiritual enlightenment, the things that bring meaning to non-saints will seem trivial to you. It's not just that the saint is giving up less important things for more important things, as though he's volunteering at a homeless shelter rather than watching TV. The things you find meaning in aren't just the things you enjoy doing; they aren't hobbies or entertainment.[7] People organize their whole lives around the things that give them meaning. They are the reasons we get out of bed in the morning, the things that define who we are, or the things we can't imagine our lives without. According to Orwell, the saint sees the vocations people find meaning in—family, music, or philosophy—as not worth caring about. The family life that Harilal yearns for is insipid, trivial, or lesser in Gandhi's eyes. The saint isn't just making different choices from the rest of us. He has a radically different orientation toward human life because he doesn't find meaning in it the same way we do. If we believe that the saint's life is best, Orwell thinks we're not really appreciating the value of being human.

You might not think of yourself as aspiring to be a saint, but the idea that our negative emotions are obstacles to a good life—that they are weeds that need to be pulled up at the root—involves the same kind of reasoning that Orwell objects to. The best kind of emotional life, so this reasoning goes, is one that has no bad feelings in it. We would all be better people if we felt less anger, jealousy, or spite. This kind of emotional sainthood is hard and few people achieve it, but we should still aspire to it. Even if we can't manage to get rid of bad feelings completely, a little bit of emotional sainthood is better than none. But this is a mistake. We shouldn't want to be emotional saints at all, not even a little. Trying to be an emotional saint means trying to be less human.

There are a variety of ways to be an emotional saint. The first version is the Controlled Emotions Saint. These saints think our bad feelings are like the weeds in the garden: not only should we pull them up at the root, we should salt the earth so they don't grow back. We need to transcend our negative emotions and feel them as little as possible or (best case scenario) not feel them at all. It might sound like a radical solution, but the history of philosophy has plenty of Controlled Emotions Saints. You might be more familiar with their contemporary successors.

Contemporary Controlled Emotions Saints

Stoicism is a philosophical tradition that is over 2,000 years old, but it has made quite a comeback in the 21st century. New Stoicism (as I'll call it) is a popular movement spearheaded by philosophers as well as nonphilosophers that draws on this ancient philosophical tradition. There are several recent popular books written by philosophers that try to teach people to live like the Stoics. New Stoicism has become particularly influential in the business world. Former American Apparel marketing director Ryan Holiday has written books about how to achieve success through Stoicism, and his work is popular among software engineers and CEOs in Silicon Valley.[8] There is even a New Stoicism conference called Stoicon that meets in London and draws philosophers, businesspeople, and members of the public from all over the world.

The message of New Stoicism is that by living Stoic principles, you can be more creative or productive in life and in business. For example, Stoic principles are behind the concept of "fear-setting," detailed by the investor and author of *4-Hour Work Week* Tim Ferriss. Fear-setting involves writing down the things you fear and asking yourself how you will handle them if they ever come to pass. It draws on the Stoic practice of thinking about your fears so that they become familiar, and therefore less scary.[9] New Stoicism often presents Stoic ideas in small, digestible bits, or as a "lifehack"—a trick for making a tough task easier.[10] New Stoicism provides high-powered CEOs or entrepreneurs ways of managing their manic pace. It focuses on developing inner calm and resilience in the face of setbacks.

Another contemporary version of emotional sainthood is the rise of "mindfulness." Mindfulness has roots in the philosophy of the Indic tradition ("Indic" because it centers on India), Zen Buddhism, and Daoism. I'll come back to these traditions in later chapters because they have lots to say about emotions. These days, though, "mindfulness" usually refers to a watered-down or commercialized version of the ideas associated with these traditions. The philosopher and expert on Buddhism Evan Thompson has dubbed it "mindfulness mania."[11] Mindfulness is often pitched as a stress reduction technique. Practices of meditation, for example, are supposed to help you find peace of mind amidst the busyness of your daily life. Like New Stoicism, mindfulness has taken off in the business world. Corporate "wellness" initiatives are supposed to help employees manage stress or burnout.[12] Many corporate wellness programs try to incorporate meditation or yoga into their daily office culture, both of which are borrowed from the Indic and Buddhist traditions.

Technology is a major player in the mindfulness game. There are countless apps, some of which offer corporate subscriptions, that help coach people through their negative feelings. As Thompson points out, neuroscientists and psychologists who have studied mindfulness have helped increase its mass appeal.[13] Take, for example, Emotional Brain Training (EBT). EBT is a mental health improvement program that promises to give its users control over their "emotional brain." According to EBT, our negative emotions cause undue stress and unhappiness—they are "faulty messengers that activate strong drives for common excesses and maladaptive states."[14] Download the EBT app and collect "joy points" when you complete the exercises. Eventually you'll train yourself out of your bad feelings.

Ecclesiastes 1:9 tells us that there is nothing new under the sun. This is true when it comes to most ideas in philosophy, and it's certainly true of the Controlled Emotions Saints. New Stoicism and mindfulness mania owe their existence to long-dead philosophers who first articulated the core ideas behind the popular movements.

The Stoics

The Stoics—not the CEOs who embrace New Stoicism, but the ancient thinkers who inspire them—are some of the most famous Controlled Emotions Saints. Stoicism arose in roughly the 3rd or 4th century BC. The original Stoics got their name from the place where they met—the *stoa poikile*, a colonnade that was next to the *agora* (the marketplace) in Athens.[15] Imagine a group of philosophers meeting regularly in Times Square: Stoics liked to be where the action was.[16] Part of the reason for this was because many of the Stoics thought that you shouldn't try to hide from the problems of the world. You need to learn how to face them, but without getting tangled in them. The Stoics think that your negative emotions are signs that you've tied yourself in knots.

One of the hallmarks of Controlled Emotions Saints is that their ideas about emotions are closely connected to their ideas about the nature of the whole universe. Understanding the Stoics' views about emotions requires knowing a little bit about how they see the world.[17] Many ancient philosophers shared a basic assumption: living things have souls and their souls are what make them alive. Souls are what some ancient philosophers called an "animating principle." In the current day and age, we tend to think souls are immaterial—they aren't like physical objects that you can see or touch. Ancient philosophers don't follow our rules. The Stoics thought souls were made out of a special kind of matter called *pneuma* (the Greek word literally means "breath"). Like your blood, *pneuma* flows through your whole body.[18] For the Stoics, human beings are a microcosm of the way the whole universe works. Just as your soul animates your body and makes you alive, the Stoics believed God (this would be the ancient Greek god, Zeus) animated the world. God was made of a special kind of *pneuma*—the Stoics called it a "designing fire"—that flowed throughout the whole cosmos and everything in it.[19]

Since God was inside the cosmos, he brought a logical or natural order to the universe, kind of like an internal blueprint. The designing fire of God told acorns to grow into oak trees and salmon to spawn upstream. Even though acorns, salmon, and people all have the same designing fire inside them, only people can actually understand the order of the cosmos and their place in it.[20] Living well for the Stoics requires that we participate correctly in this logical order. We do that by making sure we have true beliefs about it. The person who achieves the perfect ordering of their true beliefs is called a sage.

Having perfectly ordered beliefs about the cosmos transforms your emotional life. Most of what we would call emotions fall under the Stoics' term, *pathē*, which means something like "affectedness" (your *pneuma* is the thing being affected).[21] According to the Stoics, we feel emotions because we have judged something we encounter in the world to be good or bad.[22] When my nation loses a sea battle, I'm disappointed because I think winning sea battles is good. The problem, at least for some of the Stoics, is that sea battles aren't *really* good.[23] The only thing that is actually good is knowing your place in the cosmos and having perfectly ordered true beliefs.[24] Sea battles and other things like them are what the Stoics call external or natural objects: they are just part of the fabric of the world.[25] Sea battles aren't good or bad in themselves; they merely unfold as the designing fire dictates. Human beings *think* they are good or bad because we attach importance to them. When I attach importance to external objects,

I am allowing something outside of me, over which I have no control, to determine my mental state.

Here's what Epictetus, one of the Stoics from the 1st or 2nd century AD, would say to me when I'm sad about the sea battle:

> You can confidently say that no man is free if someone else has the power to obstruct and compel him. And don't consider his family tree or investigate whether he was bought or sold . . .if you hear him say "Poor me, what things I suffer," call him a slave. In short, if you see him wailing, complaining, and unhappy, call him a slave in official dress.[26]

Epictetus was never one to mince words (he spent the first twenty or so years of his life as a slave, so he probably didn't have much patience for whining). Allowing something outside of ourselves to determine our feelings is to allow external events to control our lives. The outcome of the sea battle isn't up to me. For Epictetus, the only thing that is actually up to me is my own mind: only I can decide what to believe and no one can force me to believe anything.[27] A truly free person is a person who realizes this and lives accordingly. Everyone else is a slave.

If you're wondering what to do next, Epictetus has advice for you. You should start by being honest with yourself about the things you're fond of. If I know that I am fond of winning sea battles, Epictetus thinks I should remind myself that sea battles are just events in the world that I can't control. If I accept that, then I won't be sad when they don't turn out how I want. It's good to start small and then work our way up to bigger things. Eventually, Epictetus thinks we'll get to this point: "When you kiss your little child or your wife, say that you are kissing a human being. Then, if one of them dies, you will not be troubled."[28] Perhaps unsurprisingly, Epictetus was never married.

The Stoic sage won't have emotions in the traditional sense.[29] The sage has achieved *apatheia* (where we get the word "apathy") or "unaffectedness."[30] The sage has all the correct beliefs about the world. The sage knows what we can and can't control, and so knows what to be troubled by and what not to be troubled by. Sea battles are just events, wives and children die—these are just the ways of the world.

Gandhi and the Indic Tradition

Present-day versions of mindfulness draw inspiration from the Indic philosophical tradition. The Indic tradition is rich and varied. It can be divided into two main branches: Hindu philosophy and Buddhist philosophy. We'll start with Hindu philosophy, and the Buddhists will join us in a later chapter. Since Orwell uses Gandhi as his model for the saint, we'll take a closer look at Gandhi's philosophical views.

Mohandas Gandhi ("Mahātmā" is an honorific name that was bestowed on him later) was born in 1869 in Porbandar in the Indian state of Gujarat.[31] He was raised Hindu and his mother was quite devout. In Gujarat, there was a large community of Hindus known as the Jains. They were ascetics and his mother had a close affiliation with them. At the time, India was under British colonial rule. Gandhi has vivid memories of his father's dealings with the colonial government: he recalls his father's anger and disgust at having to wear European-style dress when the governor of Bombay came to visit the city. In his late teens, Gandhi was sent to London for an education in law. While in London he joined a group called the Theosophical Society, which studied Buddhist and Hindu texts. Even though Gandhi was raised Hindu, it was in this society that he first read the *Bhagavad Gita* (the Gita, for short).

Written sometime between the 3rd century BC and the 4th century AD, the Gita is one of the central texts in Hinduism. It is a part of the *Mahābhārata*, which is an epic poem about the wars between two clans fighting over control of the kingdom of northern India.[32]

The Gita is a dialogue between two primary characters: Arjuna and Krishna. Arjuna is one of the greatest warriors in the kingdom, and Krishna is his advisor and charioteer. Krishna, it turns out, is also divine, though not all of the characters in the epic seem to know it. When the Gita opens, Arjuna and Krishna are about to go into battle, but Arjuna has a moment of crisis. Looking across the battlefield, he sees his kinsmen—fathers, sons, cousins, and uncles.[33] Arjuna wonders: what's the point of this battle. Are we justified in this? Despondent, Arjuna asks, "How, having killed our own people, could we be happy, Krishna?"[34] The rest of the Gita is a debate between Krishna and Arjuna over the merits of war as well as the nature of wisdom, knowledge, duty, and enlightenment.

Gandhi studied the Gita closely and even wrote his own commentary on the text.[35] He reads the Gita as giving guidance on ethical and religious questions. As a result, Gandhi thinks the battlefield where Arjuna and Krishna talk is a metaphor for the human condition.[36] The real battle is between the human who seeks higher truth and all of the impediments that will prevent him from finding it. Gandhi reads most of what Krishna says in the Gita as a description of how we are supposed to live so that we can attain this higher truth.

According to Gandhi, the main lesson of the Gita is to teach self-realization through renunciation.[37] The self that is being realized is the *ātman*, or the higher self that persists even if the body is destroyed.[38] The *ātman* is the self that can be perfected and can be the seat of higher truth. Gandhi believed that the way to realize this self is through renunciation of the physical or sensual.[39] His understanding of renunciation comes primarily from the second book of the Gita. There Arjuna asks Krishna what the wise and steadfast person will be like. Here are some of Krishna's answers:

> He whose mind is not agitated in misfortune/Whose desire for pleasures has disappeared/Whose passion, fear, and anger have departed/And whose meditation is steady, is said to be a sage

And when he withdraws completely/The senses from the objects
of the senses/As a tortoise withdraws its limbs into its shell/His
wisdom stands firm

For a man dwelling on the objects of the senses/An attachment to
them is born/From attachment, desire is born/From desire, anger
is born/From anger arises delusion[40]

Gandhi took Krishna's descriptions to heart, so he decided to
take a vow of *brahmacharya*. *Brahmacharya* is like a vow of celi-
bacy, but it involves more than just giving up sex. It's the vow
that explains all of Gandhi's discipline and restrictions. The goal
of *brahmacharya* is to weaken the power that your body, senses,
and desires have over your mind. Gandhi starts by controlling his
palate: he eats simple food, mostly uncooked and spiceless. This
helps him stop seeing food as an object of pleasure. He also fasts because food gives him energy, which makes his senses more alert. If
his senses are weakened, he can better control them.

But control of the senses and the body is not enough. Gandhi quotes
Krishna: "Physical sensations, truly, Arjuna/Causing cold, heat, pleasure
or pain/Come and go and are impermanent/So manage to endure
them, Arjuna."[41] Proper renunciation requires the right kind of attitude
toward our senses and the world outside of us. Physical sensations are
fleeting and should merely be tolerated. According to Gandhi, these
same sensations are also the cause of our negative emotions. Once we
realize that everything other than the *ātman* has no permanent existence, we will no longer feel fear or anger.[42] Likewise, we won't grieve the
loss of our loved ones because the *ātman* doesn't perish along with their
bodies.[43] The bodily discipline that Gandhi practiced was part of this
larger process of renunciation. Renunciation allows you to be, as Krishna
puts it, like the tortoise withdrawing into its shell. You are secure in your
ātman and undisturbed by anything outside of it.[44]

The Stoics and Gandhi have complex philosophical cosmologies
that lead them to their views about negative emotions. You might

see some faint echoes of them in New Stoicism and mindfulness mania, but without the big metaphysical commitments. The old schools and the new schools share an emphasis on inner control. They help you carve out space for yourself in a world that is threatening to you—either to your peace of mind or to your life. If you can't do anything about your external circumstances, maybe you can do something about your internal circumstances. Gandhi and the Stoics offer something attractive, especially to people who are trapped in situations they can't control: freedom.

Freedom from What?

The Controlled Emotions Saints think emotions threaten our control over our minds. There are more than enough examples to support them. When we're emotional, we often blow things out of proportion, act impulsively, and say things we later regret. Think of all the inanimate objects that we've used to take out our frustrations. Apologies are due to a lot of broken plates, punched walls, and kicked lawn mowers. And it's not just negative emotions that are the troublemakers. The old adage "love is blind" warns us that even love has a tendency to cloud our judgment. Sometimes it feels like we're being consumed or carried away by our emotions. When the dust settles, we're frustrated and angry with ourselves for not keeping it together. We've all been in the grip of emotions we wish desperately to be rid of. Soul-crushing grief, foolish love, bitter anger, burning envy—*I'd give anything not to feel this*, we whisper in our hopeless moments.

The Controlled Emotions Saints conclude that we're better off if we have more control over our emotions. There's something right about this. Imagine if an adult had the emotional life of a toddler. He might break down in sobbing hysterics because the car dealership didn't have the color he wanted on site or fly into a rage over a broken pencil. When we call people emotional, we usually mean it as a criticism. Sometimes it's a way of calling someone immature or unprofessional. We tell people who get upset over small things to grow up. Being an adult means keeping your feelings in check and staying calm even when you don't want to be.

The Controlled Emotions Saints also have a deeper criticism of the emotional person. People who are carried away by their feelings lack what philosophers sometimes call *agency*—our ability to think for ourselves, to choose, to make decisions, and to act in the world. The Controlled Emotions Saints will say that people who have no control over their emotional life have no control over their own agency. If I don't have control over my emotions, I can be derailed by them at any time. My agency would be pulled in different directions by them like a boat tossed by the waves. When people are emotional, we sometimes say: pull yourself together! In a way, we mean that literally. You need to get a hold on your emotions if you want to be an agent in the world. The Controlled Emotions Saints think our emotions threaten our ability to keep ourselves together and that's why we need to keep them in check.

But there's an unspoken assumption here: we're passive in the face of our emotions. They are like powerful forces that overtake us or consume us, and that's why we have to keep them at bay. But the times when we feel completely carried away by our emotions are rare. Of course, we don't decide to get angry in the same way we decide to go to the movies. Sometimes emotions are sudden: I hear a crash in the kitchen in the middle of the night and I'm instantly afraid. Sometimes they dawn on us slowly: I grow more and more frustrated the longer I have to wait in the doctor's office. Yet even when we're very afraid and very frustrated, we can usually keep our wits about us. I can be afraid without being in a full-blown panic, and I can be frustrated without making a scene in the lobby. If we were completely passive in the face of our feelings, it's hard to see how anyone would be able to talk themselves out of a feeling or calm themselves down, but we do these things all the time.

Another hidden assumption is the idea that our emotions are irrational. "Irrational" has multiple meanings.[45] Sometimes we use it when we actually mean "arational" or "nonrational." A sneeze isn't rational, but it's not irrational either: it's not the sort of thing that can be rational or irrational. Most of the time we call emotions irrational because they go against reason: your logical side says one thing, but your emotional side says the opposite. But, as we saw earlier, there are good reasons to doubt the stark divide between reason and emotion. Emotions can be logical (remember the axe murderer) and logic can be emotional, especially if we're deliberating about big life choices.

For the Controlled Emotions Saints, however, emotions are irrational in a different way. Emotions, especially negative ones, are like optical illusions or false beliefs. We feel them because something about the way we're seeing our lives or the world is mistaken. If we correct the mistakes, the emotions will go away (maybe permanently). The Stoics will say that our strong emotions arise because we have false beliefs about what's important or what's in our control. For Gandhi, negative emotions are like a delusion. We feel them because we wrongly believe that the world has permanence that it doesn't really have. Our emotions reflect or reveal what we care about, and the Stoics and Gandhi would argue that this is the root of the problem. Negative emotions show that we are too invested in the world or that we're invested in the wrong things. The Controlled Emotions Saints think correcting our false beliefs about the nature of the world is the key to getting rid of our negative emotions. Once we understand how the world really is, our emotional life will follow suit and we'll no longer be led astray by our feelings—that's why their views about the universe are central to the ways they think about emotions. Correct your beliefs about how the world is and you'll correct your feelings. As Gandhi puts it, "We feel afraid only so long as we take the rope to be a serpent."[46]

But why are the Stoics and Gandhi so sure about this? The fiction writer George Eliot explores this very question in her novella *The*

Lifted Veil.[47] The main character (Latimer) becomes ill. After his illness, he suddenly has the power of foresight: he can both read people's thoughts and can see the future. He knows that his life's course is set for him, yet Latimer is anything but at peace. He sees in his visions a terrible future for himself, but he can't stop hoping that it will be better than it actually seems. He is moody, resentful, and sensitive to everything. Eventually, he fixes the problem by just avoiding people. The more he isolates himself, the calmer he gets. He starts to feel more connected to the constellations and to distant mountains than he does to his friends and family. Latimer isn't happy, peaceful, or enlightened. He's distant, isolated, and can barely be in the same room with other humans. Knowing the truths of the universe is supposed to bring you inner peace, but what if it doesn't? What if it turns you into someone who no longer knows how to be around real people?

The Controlled Emotions Saints think we're better off diminishing our investment in the living, breathing human world around us. We should care about it less, and if we manage that, we won't be plagued by negative emotions. They make the choice that Orwell thinks we shouldn't make. They reorient themselves so that they no longer see human life as meaningful in the same way regular humans do. Is it worth it? Is it worth living like a tortoise in its shell just so we can avoid bad feelings?

A Tortoise, but Halfway Out?

The contemporary versions of the Controlled Emotions Saints try to achieve peace of mind without the underlying commitments to radically different views of the universe. You might think we don't have to go all in with Gandhi or the Stoics, but a little bit of sainthood will go a long way. Negative emotions are trouble, and we should curb them even if we don't take vows of *brahmacharya*. Can we reap the benefits of sainthood without changing our worldviews completely?[48]

I've often wondered what the Stoics would think of the rise of New Stoicism. Some of them would probably be happy that more people are trying to practice it. Some of them (I like to think Epictetus would be one) would probably be horrified. For many of the Stoics, the idea of trying to become a sage without believing in their cosmology is like trying to be a priest without believing in God. Sages are sages because they have well-ordered beliefs about the nature of the universe—accepting the comprehensive doctrine is necessary for the personal transformation. The same is true of Gandhi. Realization of your higher self depends on renunciation. Proper renunciation requires you to believe in the impermanence of the physical world and the existence of the *ātman*. The Controlled Emotions Saints's views about the universe are central to their plans for living well. You can't correct your emotions without them.

Why are we so hesitant to take the tough metaphysical therapy that the Controlled Emotions Saints offer? Let me start with a jaundiced answer. There's a German term that philosophers use that means a dominant idea or tendency in public life: *zeitgeist*. There's a pro-positivity *zeitgeist* all around us, and I think most of the popularity of New Stoicism and mindfulness mania is a reflection of it. The *zeitgeist* gained momentum in the 1950s with the best-selling book by Norman Vincent Peale, called *The Power of Positivity*.[49] Peale was a businessman and a minister who was part of a religious movement called the prosperity gospel. The prosperity gospel sprang out of evangelical Christianity and teaches its believers that they can harness divine power through positive affirmation.[50] In other words, if you have a strong enough faith and pray hard enough, God will quite literally deliver to you all the things you want for your life, including wealth, health, and success. The prosperity gospel has been secularized and popularized as "positive thinking" by Peale and others who came after him. One of the more recent versions is the best-selling book *The Secret* by Rhonda Byrne, which repackaged the prosperity gospel as the "law of attraction."[51] Positive thinking has been wildly influential. You see it everywhere from gyms to boardrooms to social media feeds. These days, you'll hear people talking about "manifesting" their goals.[52] No matter where you find it, the message of positive thinking has always been the same: good thoughts and feelings will make good things happen to you. If you have negative thoughts and feelings, bad things will happen.

Underlying positive thinking is the idea that nothing in our lives escapes our control. For many people, that's a comforting message. Rather than accept that bad things happen to people for no reason, positive thinking tries to convince you that all the power is in your hands. All you have to do is change your attitude. I suspect that some of the attraction of mindfulness mania and New Stoicism is actually just positive thinking under a different guise. Both the Stoics and Gandhi emphasize mental control as part of their metaphysical therapy. Although they wouldn't advocate for anything like a prosperity gospel, it's easy for people who are already caught up in the pro-positivity *zeitgeist* to filter these philosophers through its sieve. If I can just be "zen" enough, all my problems will disappear.

Part of the reason that the pro-positivity *zeitgeist* is so attractive is because of the expectation we have for how our lives should go. Psychologists Todd Kashdan and Robert Biswas-Diener call it the "rise of the comfortable class."[53] The comfortable class's vision of a good life is a life that is happy and comfortable—like spending all your days in a soft leather recliner. A happy and comfortable life, according to this picture, is one that is completely free from struggle, stress, and negativity. That, of course, includes bad feelings. For some people, New Stoicism and mindfulness mania seem to promise a shortcut (a lifehack) to a happy and comfortable life.

The question we have to ask is: why should life be like an easy chair? We will all encounter pain, frustration, and heartbreak at some point. That may sound obvious to you, but the expectation that we shouldn't be angry, fearful, or depressed is a powerful one. Just think about how many times you've experienced painful feelings and someone has told you to "cheer up" or "look at the bright side." You tell someone about a hardship you've suffered, and they respond with "it could have been worse." When we're angry, we hear "be the bigger person" or "calm down" or "don't waste your energy." You've been told your bad feelings are "unhealthy" or "unproductive." Negative emotions have been compared to poisons, toxins, monsters, or cancers. If you don't stop feeling them quickly, they'll eat you up from the inside. Even when people admit that you can't completely avoid frustration or heartbreak, they're hesitant to let anyone feel the pain of it for very long.

Not everyone involved in New Stoicism or mindfulness mania is being strung along by the pro-positivity *zeitgeist*, and the original Stoics and Gandhi certainly weren't on board with it. One of the main attractions of the Controlled Emotions Saints is that they push you to have perspective.[54] When we encourage people to have perspective, we're asking them to have a sense of significance or proportion. Worry about the big stuff, but don't sweat the small stuff. Many of our negative emotions appear to be the result of a lack of perspective. Envy is a prime example. We usually associate envy with materialism: you're too focused on having the nicest house on the block with the nicest car in the driveway. Anger falls prey to this criticism, too. We have a tendency to make every minor slight or frustration into a grave injustice. Someone cuts me off in traffic or I have a run-in with my least favorite coworker and I proclaim that my day is ruined and the universe is out to get me. Many people think the root cause of many of our bad feelings is taking unimportant things too seriously.

But that means the target of the criticism isn't the emotions themselves. The emotions are just symptoms of a bigger problem: the lack of perspective or caring about the wrong things. When we criticize people for envying the neighbor's car, what we're really saying is that material things aren't important. We're telling people to stop valuing houses and cars or to value them less. When we criticize people for being too angry over traffic, we're saying that traffic isn't worth getting upset about. Caring about cars is shallow and being angry at traffic is petty. We say we're criticizing negative emotions, but we're really being critical of what people care about or how much they care about it.

Of course, we can get too wrapped up in silly things, and we can make mountains out of molehills. But having perspective and getting rid of bad feelings aren't as connected as they might seem. It's good to not sweat the small stuff, but what do we think sweating the big stuff looks like? Unless you are the full-blooded version of a Controlled Emotions Saint, the fact that you have a sense of proportion or significance won't rule out negative emotions entirely. Change the anger example a little: say my least favorite coworker slashes my tires. Being angry about that is not sweating the small stuff. In the same way that my fear of the axe murderer is telling me that I'm in danger, my anger over the tires is telling me that I've been mistreated. Slashed tires are worth getting upset about. We can have proper perspective and still be susceptible to negative emotions.

For the ardent Controlled Emotions Saints, most things in human life are molehills (add slashed tires to the list with sea battles). These saints don't distinguish between petty human interests and regular human interests. Gandhi and the Stoics thought we should care less about friends and family, not just traffic jams or the neighbor's new car. The central claim of the Controlled Emotions Saints is that inner calm, peace of mind, and freedom require us to be less invested in ourselves and our lives. We're supposed to be keeping all the things we can't control at arm's length. When we free ourselves from these concerns, we carve out psychic space that is completely ours. It's what protects us from getting too tangled up in the problems of the world. No matter what comes our way, we remain unaffected like the tortoise in its shell.

The Stoics and Gandhi are right about something: being suscep-tible to negative emotions means you are invested in and attached to your life and the world. What they see as a negative, Orwell and I see as a positive. What it means to be human is to be fully entangled in your life and vulnerable to it. The Controlled Emotions Saints and their contemporary popular versions try to resist getting caught up in the messiness of human life. But the mess *is* your life. Trying to get rid of the mess is trying to not be human anymore.

By now I hope you'll agree that living well, complete with your negative emotions, doesn't require this kind of sainthood. Maybe you're convinced that the Controlled Emotions Saints are asking too much, but it's tempting to think that we need to do *something* about our bad feelings. Don't they cause us all kinds of pain? Don't they end up hurting other people? If these questions are nagging you, there's another version of the emotional saint you need to meet.

2

Taming the Beasts

Busytown, a fictional world created by children's author Richard Scarry, is a town full of anthropomorphic animals. Residents of Busytown include Huckle the Cat, who is the main character in the stories, Rudolf von Flugel, the fox who owns a hot air balloon, and Bruno the Bear, who runs the snack stand at Busytown Beach. There's also Lowly Worm, the earthworm who is Huckle's friend. Lowly Worm is Busytown's only invertebrate character; all the other residents are mammals, reptiles, or birds. Like the other characters, Lowly Worm does human things. He wears clothes (a green hat, a blue shirt, a bowtie, and one red sneaker) and drives a car (it looks like a giant apple with wheels). He is a model citizen: he recycles, has excellent table manners, and helps Huckle find a birthday present for his mother.[1] How does Lowly Worm blend into Busytown so seamlessly despite being the only worm? Maybe it's because he's cultivated. Unlike regular worms who squirm around in the dirt, he has cleaned himself up and made himself presentable. He has transformed himself into a worm fit for the society of Busytown.

The next group of emotional saints treat your negative emotions like Lowly Worm. I call them the Cultivated Emotions Saints. Contemporary emotional cultivation goes by names such as "emotional management," "emotional intelligence," or "emotional regulation."[2] The Cultivated Emotions Saints are less suspicious of emotions than the Controlled Emotions Saints. For these saints, the solution to bad feelings is not to root them out or stamp them down. Instead, we should cultivate or transform them so that they stop causing trouble.

How are we supposed to train our feelings? The Cultivated Emotions Saints reject the idea that our emotions are irrational forces that just crash down on us. They are more like our talents and tastes, which can be improved with the right kinds of interventions. One set of interventions works from, as Nancy Sherman puts it, "the outside in."[3] You've probably heard the phrase "dress for success." This is an outside-in strategy: if you dress like a professional, you'll supposedly feel like a professional. The famed "gratitude practice" from positive psychology is another outside-in intervention. Make a list of all the things you're thankful for or take a few minutes every day to count your blessings. These practices are supposed to help you develop a grateful mindset, which, according to positive psychology research, will make you happier and healthier.[4] How do you train a child to feel remorse about hurting their sibling? Force them to apologize and point out how sad baby brother is because of what they did. The words come first (usually begrudgingly), and the feelings show up later.

Another type of intervention is what I'll call "space-making." Space-making puts a little bit of distance between you and your feelings. It's the tool that people usually recommend for dealing with negative emotions. It forces you to stop and reflect on your feelings before you act on them. You've probably heard of strategies such as counting to ten, taking deep breaths, or typing up a scathing email you won't actually send. Space-making interventions prevent us from acting impulsively, which tends to be a problem with negative emotions. They also give us a chance to ask ourselves whether our emotions are appropriate for the situation: am I just overreacting to my least favorite coworker's comment? The Cultivated Emotions Saints think that the key to living well with our bad feelings is to train them to be better, and these strategies are part of the training.

Like the Controlled Emotions Saints, the Cultivated Emotions Saints have a long history in philosophy. Long before we started talking about emotional intelligence, Confucius and Aristotle had plenty of advice to give about how to cultivate your feelings.

Confucius

The person known to most of the Western world as Confucius was known to his followers as Kongzi or Master Kong (*zi* 子 means "master").[5] Jesuit missionaries in China Latinized his name as Confucius in the 17th century. Confucius lived from about 551–479 BC in the state of Lu during the decline of the Zhou Dynasty. Zhou rule was similar to feudal Europe: the king controlled various fiefdoms, which were governed by lords. Trouble started when barbarian tribes sacked the Zhou capital in 770 and the royal family was forced to move the capital city farther east. The feudal lords began to take advantage of the weakness of the king and to usurp royal authority for themselves. The state of Lu and Confucius himself, however, remained loyal to the Zhou.

Confucius's ideas are found primarily in the *Analects* (also known as *Lunyu*, which means "ordered sayings"). It's supposed to be a collection of his teachings compiled by his disciples, although the authorship and date of the text are disputed. Confucius had once been a public official, and as part of his job he was expected to ensure that traditional state rituals were followed.[6] Since he knew these rituals and the texts that detailed them, young men with political aspirations would seek his advice. Confucius's advice comes from his comprehensive philosophical doctrine, which is often described as following "the Way" or the *Dao* (道). It means "path" or "road." Confucius's *Dao* is not to be confused with Daoism, which is a rival philosophical school to Confucianism (the two schools disagree about what the Way looks like and how we follow it).[7]

Following the Confucian Way involves self-cultivation, and central to it is the practice of ritual or *li* (禮). *Li* covers a wide range of activities that includes family obligations, religious sacrifices, everyday good manners, and the duties of public office.[8] *Li* dictates, for example, how to bury your parents when they die, but it also tells you where to store sacred tortoises used for divination.[9] Confucius's focus on the importance of ritual sometimes makes him look like a stickler for rules, but *li* means more than that. To get a sense of how it works, think about learning a specific dance, like a waltz. There are certain requirements you have to follow in order for the dance to count as waltzing (rather than, say, break-dancing). When you're first learning the steps, you're anchored to specifics such as maintaining your posture, moving your feet, and keeping time in your head. You're focused on following all the "rules" of the waltz.

If you are constantly conscious of counting in your head and thinking about your feet, you won't be very good at waltzing. Once you get past the basics, you're supposed to be absorbed in the dance—feeling the music and gliding across the floor. Now you are really waltzing. The same is true of *li*. Engaging in rituals and rites isn't just following all the right steps; you have to feel the ritual and understand its importance. According to Confucius, observing *li* properly transforms you into a fully fledged person.[10] It's one of the ways we become *ren* (仁), which means "good" or "humane." Becoming *ren* is what Confucian self-cultivation is aiming for. The person who is *ren* will move through the world *wu-wei* (無為) or with a kind of effortless action.[11] She does what *li* requires with sincerity and spontaneity.

Becoming *ren* includes feeling the right emotions, including negative emotions. Confucius tells his disciples, "Only one who is Good (*ren*) is able to truly love or despise others."[12] It may sound odd to claim that a good person will despise other people, but Confucius thinks some things are rightly despicable. "Glibness" or *ning* (佞), which literally means "beautiful of speech," is one of those things. Glib people are those who might follow ritual closely and give the appearance of being *ren*, but who are just going through the motions. Confucius describes glibness by posing questions such as, "If someone seems sincere and serious in their conversation, does this mean they are a gentleman? Or have they merely adopted the appearance of the gentleman?"[13] Glib people are good at faking it, but they don't have the proper emotions that are supposed to accompany *li*. According to Confucius, if you love and honor what is *ren*, you also hate those things that are the opposite of *ren*. People who are *ren* don't abstain from hate altogether; they just train themselves to hate the right things.

The *ren* person feels exactly the right emotion at the right time in a way that is sincere and unforced but also appropriate. Confucius's comments on grief give us the best illustration. Readers of the *Analects* know that Yan Hui is Confucius's favorite pupil. Confucius praises his virtue constantly and tells his other students how unlike Yan Hui they are. Sadly, Yan Hui dies young and Confucius is devastated. He cries out, "Heaven has bereft me! Heaven has bereft me!"[14] He weeps so much that eventually his disciples ask whether he's being a bit excessive. Confucius responds: "Am I showing excessive grief? Well, for whom would I show excessive grief, if not for this man?"[15] Confucius's point is that a great loss—the untimely death of your favorite student—is the right time for great sorrow. Your grief should always fit the occasion.

To be *ren* is to feel both positive and negative emotions but to feel them with sincerity at the right time and in the right way. Just as the master of the waltz glides across the floor, fully immersed in the music, the *ren* person feels all the right emotions in *wu-wei* fashion—effortlessly, spontaneously, and yet always within the proper bounds.

Aristotle

Aristotle, whom we met briefly in the Introduction, was born in Macedonia in roughly 384 BC (about 100 years after Confucius died).[16] In 367, when he was 17, he moved to Athens to join Plato's school (called the Academy). When Plato died in 347, Aristotle went back to Macedonia and served as a tutor for Alexander, the son of King Philip, who would eventually become known as Alexander the Great. Aristotle returned to Athens in 335 to open his own philosophical school known as the Lyceum. He lived and taught there until 323 when his ties to the Macedonian royal family made life difficult for him. Alexander had by this time become king and spent most of his days trying to conquer Persia and quashing any signs of political rebellion, including in Athens. Anti-Macedonian attitudes in Athens were strong, and Aristotle took the hint. He moved to an island in northern Greece where he could study fish (one of his long-time interests) and died there in 322.

The two works in which Aristotle talks the most about emotions are the *Nicomachean Ethics* and the *Rhetoric*. In these works, he argues that all human beings aim at *eudaimonia*, which is often translated as "flourishing." Like Confucius, Aristotle thinks flourishing requires self-cultivation.[17] He refers to this process as trying to achieve "excellences of character."[18] The excellences of character are what we would normally call good character traits or virtues: qualities such as honesty, courage, or generosity. We develop the excellences of character through what Aristotle calls "habituation,"[19] that is, learning by doing, in the same way you learn the waltz by practicing it again and again. Habituation is responsible for both our good and bad character traits.[20] Aristotle often compares habituation to learning to play a musical instrument: if you practice the tuba well, you'll become a good tuba player, but if you practice it badly, you'll be a bad tuba player. To acquire the right traits, you have to repeat and practice the right kinds of actions.

According to Aristotle, many of the excellences of character involve regulating our emotions and striking a balance between two extremes. Aristotle identifies one of the character excellences as "mildness," and it lies between the extremes of too much and too little anger.[21] In the *Rhetoric*, Aristotle defines anger as a response to "an apparent slight that was directed, without justification, against oneself or those near to one."[22] We're most often angry when someone insults us or treats us disrespectfully. Aristotle describes the person who doesn't feel enough anger as "foolish," "insensate," and "slavish."[23] People who feel too little anger seem unable to recognize when they are being treated unjustly, or they are unwilling to stand up for themselves. If the guy at the end of the bar starts saying untoward things about your mother and you do nothing about it, Aristotle would say you're either foolish or weak. Anger is the right response to mistreatment, and the person with the excellence of mildness will feel it appropriately.[24]

The person who feels the right emotions at the right time and in the right way has *phronesis*, which is typically translated as "practical wisdom." Having *phronesis* means knowing what different situations call for and doing those things when the time is right.[25] The practically wise person doesn't just do the right thing at the right time; they also feel the right way at the right time.

Practice Makes Perfect

For those who sense something alien about the Controlled Emotions Saints, the Cultivated Emotions Saints seem like a return to Earth. The Cultivated Emotions Saints recognize the importance of emotions in a good life. Surely, they will say, there is something wrong with the person who doesn't grieve the untimely death of his favorite student or the person who isn't angry at the disrespectful thug in the bar. For the Cultivated Emotions Saints, living well means feeling well.

There's something familiar about this. Think about all the ways we judge each other (including ourselves) for our emotional responses. Imagine being away for a long work trip, and when you come home, your spouse seems indifferent to your return. "Did he even miss me?" you wonder. Suppose you're watching some horrific tragedy on the evening news and your friend laughs it off. "That's so callous," you might think. Perhaps you hear that your least favorite coworker is in trouble with the boss. Your first response may be an evil grin, which then probably gives way to a pang of shame. "Come on," you say to yourself, "don't enjoy someone else's pain." We don't restrict our judgments about others and ourselves just to actions or choices. What people feel or don't feel matters to us. The Cultivated Emotions Saints can easily make sense of emotional criticism because they think emotions accompany our traits or thoughts. Possessing the right traits and having the right thoughts means that you will have the right emotional responses.

In the last chapter, we talked briefly about having agency with our emotions. We think there's something wrong with the person who flies into a rage or breaks down sobbing over something small. The Cultivated Emotions Saints give us a way of having agency without getting rid of our emotions. We can train our feelings so that they are always appropriate for the circumstances. If I find myself getting frustrated with the long wait at the doctor's office I can remind myself that everyone in the situation is doing the best they can or that a long wait is not a big deal. These kinds of interventions will help me calm down in the moment, but they'll also help me shape my emotional responses in the future. Over time, I can get better at identifying which situations call for different levels of anger. A long wait at the doctor only calls for a little anger, whereas someone saying untoward things about my mother might call for more. Having appropriateness in the forefront of our minds helps us develop the kind of emotional agency we're looking for.

Even though the Cultivated Emotions Saints defend our feelings, there are still some emotions that can't be improved. For example, there's no right way or right time to feel envy. According to Confucius, rather than envying others who are more accomplished, the *ren* person will "concentrate on becoming their equal" and "look within" themselves to see how they can improve.[26] Aristotle argues that envy is the result of a malicious character and that malice is "combined with badness from the start."[27] Luckily, the Cultivated Emotions Saints can argue that there aren't that many of these bad feelings. Most of our emotions, including some of the negative ones, are important parts of a good life. They just need a little training to make sure they don't get out of hand.

Chautauqua Lake

William James, the American 19th-century philosopher whom we met briefly in the Introduction, gave a series of lectures to a group of teachers in the early 1900s. In one of these lectures, he tells a story about visiting Chautauqua Lake, a lakeside resort in upstate New York.[28] It was sort of like a summer camp with cultural programming and was originally founded to provide training for Sunday School teachers.[29] James describes the setting as idyllic: "Sobriety and industry, intelligence and goodness, orderliness and ideality, prosperity and cheerfulness, pervade the air."[30] There is a chorus, educational lectures, a gym, and "perpetually running soda-water fountains."[31] Chautauqua Lake provides all the wholesome fun, enrichment, and recreation that anyone could ask for. When his week-long stay is up, James describes how he feels leaving the lake:

> Ouf! what a relief! Now for something primordial and savage. . . . This human drama without a villain or a pang; this community so refined that ice-cream soda-water is the utmost offering it can make to the brute animal in man . . . this atrocious harmlessness of all things—I cannot abide with them. Let me take my chances again in the big outside worldly wilderness with all its sins and sufferings. There are the heights and depths . . . the gleams of the awful and the infinite; and there is more hope and help a thousand times than in this dead level and quintessence of every mediocrity.[32]

My reaction to the Cultivated Emotions Saints is a little bit like James's reaction to Chautauqua Lake. There is something missing from the orderly emotional life that Confucius and Aristotle think we should create—it's too wholesome, too neat. They think we need to train our feelings so that they always follow the standards of appropriateness. It's fine to feel anger, they will say, as long as it's not too strong or at the wrong time or in the wrong way. The Cultivated Emotions Saints think our feelings can be tamed, but I'm not sure they can be. And, even if they can, I'm not sure they should be. We should prefer them wild.

Both groups of emotional saints are trying to solve the practical problem of emotions: how do we live with a part of our inner mental life that we can't completely control? The Controlled Emotions Saints think we do this by diminishing the power of our emotions—make them weaker and you can control them better. The Cultivated Emotions Saints, by contrast, think we should work with rather than against our emotions—we just have to train them. Maybe you can't control your feelings directly, but you can control them indirectly. The strategies of emotional cultivation are supposed to help us do this. You can't decide to feel gratitude, but you can decide to write down what you're thankful for or remind yourself of all the good things in your life. The Cultivated Emotions Saints think that if we act the right way and make the right choices, the right emotions will follow along—as though they are tethered together. Once I judge anger to be the right response in a situation, the appropriate amount of anger is supposed to appear.

But our emotions don't play by these rules. People can think all the right thoughts and make all the right choices, but the emotions don't just follow along. We have too many examples of people who have tried and failed to make themselves to feel something or to stop feeling something. Think all the right thoughts, make all the right choices, and your feelings betray you anyway. Our feelings have a life of their own; that's what makes them a practical problem in the first place. In moments when your feelings betray you, you *wish* you had the kind of control over your emotions that Confucius and Aristotle think you do. Sometimes you wish you could stop yourself from feeling anything at all. The Cultivated Emotions Saints might claim that people in such situations just haven't done a good enough job of training their feelings, but no matter how much training we do, our control will never be total.

But it's not just that we can't fully train our feelings. We shouldn't want to.

W. E. B. Du Bois was an American philosopher who lived during the late 19th and early 20th centuries and studied with William James at Harvard. Like Anna Julia Cooper, who was his contemporary, he wrote about what it was like to be Black in America. One of the essays in his most famous collection, *The Souls of Black Folk*, is about the death of his first-born child. Du Bois describes all the emotional turmoil of his grief. He accuses Death of taking his baby's life because it was "jealous of one little coign of happiness" that Du Bois had with his son.[33] He tries to convince himself that his son is better off and that he's in heaven, but the most he can muster is a meek wish that "if he is There . . . let him be happy."[34] On the day of the burial, Du Bois describes "an awful gladness" in his heart at the thought that his son will never face the pain and horror of racism in America—a voice inside him says of his son, "Not dead, not dead, but escaped; not bond, but free."[35] Du Bois asks Death: why not me? He writes, "Why may I not rest me from this restlessness?"[36] There is ambiguity in his words: interpreted one way, Du Bois is asking why he couldn't have died instead because he has already had time on this earth and his son didn't. Interpreted another way, he is asking: why should my son be free and not me?

It's clear that Du Bois is struggling with his feelings. He finds the "awful gladness" in his heart in spite of what he thinks he's supposed to feel. Du Bois's feelings may not meet the standard for whatever appropriate grief is supposed to look like, but they also aren't mistaken. His complicated feelings are a response to his complicated situation. Du Bois knows painfully well what it's like to live as a Black person in a racist country. He was afraid to watch his son grow up in a world that Du Bois knew would eventually reject him and even try to hurt him. If he sees his baby's death as a kind of freedom—freedom from the daily struggle of trying to build a human life under the weight of racism—it's not hard to see why Du

Bois would, even momentarily, be glad for that freedom and wish for it himself.

The Cultivated Emotions Saints argue that we can train our feelings to listen to us. When we've decided we should feel one way (the appropriate way) and yet we feel a different way, what should we do? Here is one problem with an emphasis on appropriateness: we can be wrong about what we think we should feel.[37] We know too many people who try to convince themselves they should feel something when in reality their notions of appropriateness are deluded. We also know too many people whose feelings are alerting them to something important, but they ignore them because they don't fit with whatever story they've told themselves. Du Bois's feelings reveal painful truths about his life that might be hard for him to consciously admit, acknowledge, or appreciate. He may not want to feel the awful gladness in his heart, but that gladness is a testament to exactly how difficult it is to have hope for your child's future in a country where racism dominates. It may be that finding the awful gladness in his heart is helping him realize all this. If he ignores it or chastises himself for feeling it, he's ignoring the reality his feelings are seeing.

Polishing the rough edges of our emotions comes at a cost. What we care about or what matters to us isn't always the result of the choices or decisions we make. Sometimes we discover what matters to us and our emotions play an important role in that discovery. Grief is a good illustration: we don't always know how we'll react in grief.[38] You might expect that you'll be sad, but you might instead be furious or relieved. You might expect that you'll be a little bit sad, but it turns out you're devastated. If I'm devastated by someone's death, it might mean that they were more central to my life than I acknowledged. My feelings might be part of my realization that I didn't spend as much time with them as I wanted or that I never got to tell them how much they meant to me. Our feelings and our judgments about what is appropriate can conflict, but that doesn't mean our feelings are wrong and our judgments are right. Emotions have their own intelligence. If our feelings sometimes know better than we do, that means we have to learn how to listen to them rather than train them to listen to us. We need to learn how to let them be exactly what they are and allow them to have a life of their own.

The Cultivated Emotions Saints don't defend the raw, uncut versions of our feelings. At the end of the day, they're still saints: bad feelings can stay only if they reform. They only approve of emotions that look like Lowly Worm with perfect manners and a snappy bowtie. Lowly Worm is dapper and he's a lovely dinner guest. But except for his basic anatomy, he's lost all the things that make him a worm—no dirt, no slime. Loving worms only if they shed all their worminess isn't really loving them at all.

"The Brute Animal in Man"

You might agree that our emotions can tell us important things and that we need to let them have some independence. You might be less comfortable with the idea that this applies to some of our negative emotions, such as envy or contempt. We are steeped in the belief that negative emotions will cause chaos if we don't do something about them. All we see are bodies in the wake of jealous spouses, angry bosses, and contemptuous neighbors. We've heard over and over again how our negative emotions poison us, make us miserable, and eat us up from the inside. They cause us to hurt people and ruin our relationships. Even if none of the catastrophes come to pass, we'd still be better off if we didn't feel them. We'd be better people, more productive, or psychologically healthier.

Most of the things we say about negative emotions are just plain mistaken. They're not toxins or poisons, and they aren't going to eat you. They won't wreck your relationships, and getting over them doesn't make you a bigger or better person. Of course, there are plenty of reasons why we shouldn't always act on them, but that doesn't mean there's anything wrong with feeling or expressing them. We have good reasons not to act on our every thought, but nobody tells you to stop having thoughts. I'll come back to the question of what to do with our bad feelings in the next chapter. For now, let's try to correct some of the misperceptions people have about them.

One reason I don't think we should be suspicious of bad feelings is because they are ubiquitous. The vast majority of human beings throughout the ages and from all walks of life have felt these emotions at some point and managed to get away unscathed. When we get nervous about bad feelings, we tend to dwell on their most dramatic instances. When we think of envy, for example, some of us might think of Shakespearean villains like Iago from *Othello*, who intentionally ruins the lives of Desdemona, Othello, and Cassio because Othello promotes Cassio over him. Is Iago's real problem his envy? There's clearly more going on with Iago than his feelings. He's an evil mastermind who waffles between cold calculation and burning vengeance; he's wicked and yet eloquent. He's an enigmatic character that defies easy explanation and one of the greatest villains in literature. If Iago were just a regular person, he probably would have stewed for a while about being passed over, given Cassio an unflattering nickname that he would never say to his face, and complained to his friends at happy hour. And then he would have gotten over it and moved on with his life. That wouldn't be a very interesting play, but it's how most people deal with their envy. Iago isn't a villain because he envies Cassio. He's a villain because he is wicked, and wicked people do terrible things with their bad feelings.

The suspicion we have about bad feelings is mostly due to what I call the *emotion double standard*. The emotion double standard is at work when people attribute things to negative emotions that they would never attribute to positive emotions. Here's just one example: people say negative emotions are like drugs, and you'll get addicted to them if you feel them too much. No one warns you against getting addicted to joy or gratitude. If negative emotions have an addictive property, why don't positive emotions have it too? Of course, some proponents of positive psychology might argue that you can get addicted to positive emotions, but they'll tell you that's a good thing. Addiction isn't the problem; you just need to get hooked on the right drug.

Is it true that good feelings never cause trouble? Love can become obsessive, possessive, and consuming. You might be tempted to say that love isn't the real culprit here, that there's something else going on with someone who loves this way. But if that's right, then we can say the same thing about Iago's envy—unless, of course, you're thinking with the emotion double standard. You could object that obsessive love is not real love, but why not? Why can't positive emotions get distorted and twisted? The idea that obsessive love isn't really love is an example of what Aaron Ben Ze'ev and Ruhama Goussinsky call "romantic ideology."[39] One part of that ideology is the "purity of love," the notion that love is always innocent and sweet.[40] The idea that love can never go wrong is mythology. There are plenty of examples of people who are obsessive, foolish, and destructive with their love.[41] Despite all these instances, no one puts love on the naughty list—providing us with another example of the emotion double standard.

You might be tempted to say that the person who is addicted to joy is still better off than the person who is addicted to anger. The angry person will hurt someone, but at most the joyful person will be too chipper. Here is another instance of focusing on extreme cases: when we think of angry people, we think of someone who flies into a berserker rage. My guess is that you probably know some people you would describe as angry who don't do this. Think of people like the American comedian Bill Hicks, who describes himself as "an avowed misanthrope."[42] His ranting, swearing curmudgeon onstage persona was an exaggerated version of his personality. You could describe him as abrasive and provocative, but he wasn't a raging ogre.[43]

You may have gone through prolonged periods in your life when you were angry with someone—probably even very angry—and they are still standing and so are you. Think of how common it is for family members to be angry with each other for years. You can lament that this isn't a good thing, but it also isn't necessarily pathological. Family members can be angry at each other and still interact without being at each other's throats (though holidays might be awkward). Anger like this is often hanging in the background, an emotional wallflower; it's present but not intrusive. Angry people sometimes have perfectly good reasons for being angry. Again, family relations provide great examples: the anger might stem from a legitimate conflict where neither person is overreacting and both have grounds for being mad. There are no fits of rage and no destructive behavior. Angry people can be just like the rest of us.

Why are we never suspicious of people who are blissed out on joy or compassion? We tend to think the joyful person is just happy and well adjusted, but this assumption is the result of the emotion double standard. What if the joyful person's positivity comes from a denial of reality? As we saw in the last chapter, such a person could be a disciple of the prosperity gospel or operating under the illusion of the law of attraction. Their joy might be the result of their shallowness or lack of imagination. Maybe their joy is an attempt to assert a kind of superiority over other people or a desperate attempt to exert control over a situation where no control is to be had. Positive emotions can be the subject of delusion and distortion or the result of pathologies and bad traits in the same way negative emotions can.

There is a pervasive idea that even if negative emotions don't cause destruction, we should still get rid of them for the sake of our psychological health. Bad feelings are bad emotional hygiene.[44] Of course, Confucius and Aristotle would disagree with this idea, but many of the contemporary versions of the Cultivated Emotions Saints haven't minded their elders. The self-help and wellness industries make billions of dollars trying to help people "manage their stress" or "let go of negativity," which are often code phrases for bad feelings. The reasoning goes this way: bad feelings make you feel bad.[45] You don't want to feel bad, so get rid of your bad feelings. To begin with, there's an inconsistency here. If negative emotions are like drugs and we can get addicted to them, then they have to give us at least some kind of high. Negative emotions are sometimes described as "seductive" for this reason—they're tempting or alluring somehow. They can't make us feel *that* bad. Otherwise, we'd never get hooked.

Emotional hygiene seems appealing because unfortunately many people are unhappy. They are stuck in difficult situations, and they want a way to feel better. Emotional hygiene tells you that you can feel better if you just get rid of all those feelings that are weighing you down. There's a bait-and-switch here: contemporary Cultivated Emotions Saints will start out by saying that you shouldn't get rid of your emotions—it's pointless to deny your feelings, they'll say. Yet, all their advice is about how to slowly start to "replace" your bad feelings with better positive feelings. For example, people will tell you that when you're feeling frustrated with your job, you should acknowledge your frustration, but then remind yourself that you're lucky to have a job. This perspective shift is supposed to make your feelings of frustration go away. But if there's nothing wrong with your bad feelings, why should you try to replace them? It's good to have perspective, but as we saw in the last chapter, perspective and negative emotions can happily coexist. The mere fact that you have a bad feeling doesn't mean that you're a petty or small-minded person. Having perspective doesn't mean you have to perpetually look on the bright side; that's just denying reality.

Why is it better for you to replace your bad feelings with good ones? The cynic in me says that this is the pro-positivity *zeitgeist* in yet another guise. You sometimes hear people say bad feelings are "unproductive" or they "drain your energy" or they "don't serve" you. All this talk assumes that your negative emotions are obstacles to your happiness. Emotional hygiene tells you that if you have a peaceful inner sanctum, you can deal with all the other things in your life that make you unhappy. It tells you that your circumstances are difficult only if you make them that way. The dark side of emotional cultivation is that it tries to convince you that you need to think better or work harder to get rid of your bad feelings. If you keep having them, it's your fault. But sometimes your bad feelings are telling you painful truths about the world. Maybe your constant feelings of frustration with your job or your spouse are signs that something is wrong with your situation, not with your mind.

The idea that letting go of negativity is good is supposedly supported by findings in positive psychology research.[46] According to this body of work, feeling positive emotions leads to all sorts of benefits: better health, a happier marriage, and more success at work.[47] As is often the case with psychological research, for every study coming to one conclusion there is another study that supports the opposite conclusion. People with a positive disposition, it turns out, are gullible, rely too heavily on stereotypes, and are bad at constructing good arguments.[48] What is more, some studies suggest that negative emotions can be beneficial: angry people, for example, tend to be better able to handle disappointment, are more creative, and are better at negotiating.[49]

When you hear people defending negative emotions, it's common for them to appeal to psychological, neurological, or biological research to show that bad feelings serve some kind of purpose. The idea that bad feelings evolved for a reason isn't new: Charles Darwin, the 19th-century scientist famous for formulating the theory of evolution, proposed explanations like this in his 1872 book, *The Expression of Emotions in Man and Animals*. Some people argue that fear, for instance, causes your blood to flow more freely to your large muscle groups, which makes it easier to flee from danger.[50] You're supposed to draw the conclusion that because your negative emotions evolved to help you with some natural behavior (fleeing from predators), that means they are good. Especially for people who struggle to manage their feelings, it can help to hear that your negative emotions have some evolutionary purpose. If they play some vital function in our survival, maybe we need them.

These kinds of defenses of negative emotions sound convincing in part because we're prone to think that arguments "backed by science" are irrefutable. Studies show that people are more likely to be convinced by an argument if you tell them that the conclusion is supported by a "brain scan," even if the brain scan isn't relevant to the argument.[51] The wellness industry loves to capitalize on this tendency: apps like Happify and Emotional Brain Training specifically highlight their "science-based" approach to managing negativity. We are also prone to make the assumption that "natural = good." There's a lot of ambiguity in the words "nature" or "natural." Sometimes "natural" means "something we evolved to do." This is how the argument about fear goes: we evolved to feel fear because we need to run away from danger, so fear must be good. But *everything* humans do is in some way or another the product of an evolutionary process. That includes our emotions, but it also includes, say, violence and disease. They are also the product of evolution, so they are in some sense natural to us. Even nonhuman animals do violent things and get diseases, so it's natural to them too. Yet, most people don't conclude that violence and disease are good. Sometimes "natural" means "whatever our early ancestors did." If that's what you mean, you will need to make some serious life changes. I'd advise you to sharpen your spear-throwing skills, unless you're talking about *really* early humans—they didn't even use tools. You'd better get rid of your car and throw away your clothes because your early ancestors didn't have those. They didn't have books either, so you should probably stop reading.

In these kinds of arguments, people usually cherry-pick, in a totally inconsistent way, which things are natural and therefore good. Some people say refined sugar isn't natural, so you should avoid it, but why doesn't the same reasoning apply to electricity or soap? "Natural" simply doesn't mean "good." Evolution is not a benevolent governess. It didn't "give" us negative emotions to help us out.

Traits and behaviors are selected for because they aid in species survival. We have no way to know for sure which of our traits actually helped keep us alive up to this point—maybe it'll turn out that having a pinky finger is responsible for all of human survival and the rest is just window dressing.[52] All we know for sure is that we evolved to have the emotions we actually have. It's up to us to decide what to do with them. Evolutionary arguments can sometimes help people accept their feelings rather than wish them away. I'm all in favor of accepting our negative emotions, but we don't need to chalk them up to evolution to reach that conclusion.

All this research—the studies on evolutionary psychology or the health benefits of this or that feeling—ultimately relies on a misguided way of valuing your emotions. It assumes that emotions are valuable only if they provide some sort of tangible gain: better blood pressure, an edge in the boardroom, or the ability to run from a saber-toothed tiger. Emotions are treated as a means to some other desired goal. This is partly how we got into the pro-positivity *zeitgeist* in the first place. Positive psychology was touted as a way of solving all of life's problems, so positive emotions became valuable currency: better feelings lead to a better life. To argue that negative emotions can be the same kind of currency just perpetuates this way of thinking. Treating your emotions as an instrument that you can use to attain happiness and success—or as an impediment to happiness and success—is to alienate yourself from them. Your feelings aren't tools. They're not fuel to "give you energy." They're not little butlers in your head who are supposed to "serve you." They're not clutter that needs to be cleaned out of your mental closet. They're part of your life just like worms are part of the garden.

So, what exactly am I suggesting? Are we just supposed to let our bad feelings happen? We should just leave them alone and feel them whenever we feel them? Well, yes. Exactly.

3

Make Room for the Devil

Although *Origin of the Species* is more famous, Charles Darwin was fond of his later book, *The Formation of Vegetable Mould, Through the Action of Worms, With Observations on Their Habits.*[1] When Darwin wrote the book, earthworms were considered either a garden pest or a lower organism worth little attention, but he suspected they might be more important than people realized. Through careful observation, he discovered that earthworms work like tiny ploughs. They forage for food by burrowing through the soil. As they move, they turn the soil over, loosening it and making it more hospitable to rainwater and plant roots. Their castings (read: worm poop) are rich in nutrients that plants love. Their behavior was also more complex than their simple bodies suggested. They had preferences for food: they liked green cabbage better than red.[2] They also used leaves, pebbles, twigs, and even feathers to plug the openings of their burrows. Darwin did experiments to see how the worms did this, and he discovered that they didn't grab the objects at random. Instead, they tended to grab it by the thinnest end (like the stem of a leaf) in order to more easily pull it into their holes.[3] Darwin thought that this showed some degree of intelligence, even though he admitted such a claim would "strike everyone as improbable."[4] Darwin concludes the book with a bold statement: "It may be doubted whether there are many other animals that have played so important a part in the history of the world, as have these lowly organized creatures."[5]

Darwin's reevaluation of worms didn't just show that they were good for the garden because they tilled the soil. He questioned the standard assumptions we make about which living creatures are important. Worms aren't pests and they don't just move dirt; they enrich their environment. We should have the same attitude toward metaphorical worms in the garden: our bad feelings. Look beyond their lowly appearance and actually pay attention to them. Try to understand them on their own terms and see how they enrich our lives. Adopting a Darwinian attitude will help us abandon the aspiration of emotional sainthood. In fact, we need move about as far away from sainthood as we can. It's time to make room for the devil.

The Devil's Party

The particular version of the devil I have in mind is Satan from the 17th-century epic poem *Paradise Lost* by John Milton. Satan is easily the poem's most intriguing character, and his lines are some of the most beautiful. Since *Paradise Lost* was written, readers, critics, and scholars have warred over whether Milton meant for Satan to be a hero or a villain.[6] Regardless of which side you choose, one thing is clear: Satan is emotional.

The first time Satan is mentioned in the poem, we learn what he feels: he is "stirred up with envy and revenge."[7] The Angelic War begins because of Satan's envy toward Christ, "With envy against the Son of God . . . could not bear through pride that sight."[8] Satan is wounded by the thought that God loves Christ more than the angels—specifically, more than Satan himself. Of course, Satan loses the war and is cast down to Hell. Before he addresses his fellow defeated angels, his face is full of emotion: "care sat on his faded cheek," yet under his brow is "dauntless courage and considerate pride."[9] He shows "signs of remorse and passion to behold the fellows of his crime."[10] He tries to speak three times but bursts into "tears such as angels weep."[11] In his famous speech on Mount Niphates, Satan is even more emotional. He is full of self-doubt, angry at God, and yet despairing that he no longer has God's favor. He yearns for forgiveness but is immediately disgusted by the idea of showing submission.[12] As he speaks, "each passion dimmed his face/ Thrice changed pale with ire, envy, and despair."[13] Once he catches sight of Adam and Eve in Eden, his fierce envy and jealousy reemerges. He rages that they should "enjoy bliss on bliss while I to Hell am thrust."[14]

Satan uses his negative emotions to create justifications for his actions. He turns his envy into righteous indignation and convinces the rebel angels that they shouldn't bow to the Son: Christ is their equal, not their ruler.[15] His despair becomes principled defiance against God, whom he paints as the enemy. His anger toward God becomes a mission of vengeance that he enacts on Adam and Eve. The main source of all his emotions is also his greatest sin: his pride.[16] Satan loves himself—more than he loves his fellow angels, more than his life in heaven, more than even God. He will not kneel before anyone, even if that means spending eternity on Hell's throne: "Better to reign in Hell than serve in Heaven!"[17]

Satan's emotional life is the most human thing about him. Our envy and anger might not be on the same epic scale, but he feels what we feel and he does the same things with his emotions that we do. In writing Satan as he does, Milton gets the source of our negative emotions exactly right. Satan is envious, angry, and spiteful because he loves himself. His negative emotions are expressions or manifestations of that love. In the traditional way of understanding the story, Satan's self-love is a sin—his pride is wicked and so are his negative emotions. His self-love is all-consuming. He wants to be the center of the universe and God's favorite creature. Since he can't have that, he tries to destroy everything.

Satan's self-love might be sinful, but ours doesn't have to be. Loving yourself means you care about your own human existence.[18] It means you value your life, your personal history, your hopes and dreams, and your voice in the world that belongs to you and no one else. When we think about what it means to care about something, we usually associate it only with positive emotions. We describe a caring person, for example, as kind, compassionate, and sympathetic. But caring about something doesn't just mean feeling tenderly toward it. Caring means being invested in something and allowing it to occupy a central place in your thoughts and concerns. Think of how we care for other people. You're invested in their future, their welfare, and their growth. The care you have for a loved one is expressed through a huge range of emotions. Of course, love, compassion, and sympathy will be among them, but so will anger, disappointment, and grief. Care manifests itself in all our emotions. It is as present in our compassion and sympathy as it is in our anger and grief.

Our bad feelings are expressions of our self-love—they show up because we are invested in our lives and ourselves.[19] When I envy my neighbor's beautiful house, it's because I want a house like that for my own life; it's part of how I define success for myself. When I'm angry at my least favorite coworker's snide comment, it's because I think I don't deserve to be treated like that; people can't just act like I don't matter. If I have contempt for someone, it's because I think I'm better than they are or that they aren't worth my time or attention. I'm spiteful toward those who doubt my abilities or who try to boss me around. Negative emotions are all directed toward their different particular objects (beautiful houses, snide comments, etc.), but a catalog of these objects doesn't answer the question: why do we feel these feelings *at all*? What, in other words, makes me susceptible to feelings of envy, anger, spite, or contempt in the first place? The answer is: I care about me. Milton gets this exactly right. Satan is filled to the brim with negative emotions because he is pure self-love. It's his greatest sin, but it's also one of the things that makes him sympathetic (maybe especially for those of us with rebellious streaks). In the world of *Paradise Lost*, where everything is determined by an all-powerful being and everyone plays a specific role in a carefully structured hierarchy, Satan wants to be his own creature. He can't see himself as just another angel in the heavenly host. His voice matters, *he* matters. Setting aside all the hell he causes because of it, there is nothing wrong with that.

You might think I'm being too hasty in my defense of Satan. Isn't self-love as dangerous as Milton paints it, especially because of its connection to bad feelings? Just take a look around: people are self-absorbed. They refuse to make minor sacrifices for the sake of others, they ignore people's suffering, and they always put themselves first. Too often self-love turns into pure selfishness or egoism—you *only* love yourself and at everyone else's expense. At best, many people would say, self-love is a psychological default that we have to constantly shake ourselves out of. At worst, it's exactly as all-consuming and destructive as Satan's pride. Many people think the dangerous combination of self-love and bad feelings is the root of most of our problems. No group of philosophers captures those arguments better than the Buddhists.

The Enemy Within

There's no one thing that counts as "Buddhist philosophy."[20] Buddhist philosophers disagree with each other about many things, which is part of why it's a varied tradition, but their shared starting point is the Four Noble Truths.[21] The Truths were first articulated in the *Dharmacakrapravartana Sūtra* by Siddhārtha Gautama, the first Buddha (the title is translated as something like "Turning the Wheel of Dharma").[22] Although Gautama is the person we usually refer to when we say "The Buddha," the term *buddha* is a title given to someone who achieves the kind of enlightenment that Gautama achieved.[23] Roughly, the Four Noble Truths are: (1) Life is characterized by suffering (*duḥkha*), (2) Suffering has its origin in attachment and aversion, (3) Suffering can end, and (4) There is a knowable path to ending suffering.[24] Buddhist philosophers disagree about the finer points of all four truths, but there is general agreement that the self is one of the main sources of suffering.

Most Buddhist philosophers believe that are two ways of seeing the world: the conventional way and the real way.[25] Think of it like being in a funhouse. The conventional world is the inside of the funhouse. Most people don't even realize they're in one—they think the illusions are real life. Attaining enlightenment means escaping the funhouse (seeing the way the world really is). The first step is realizing that nothing in the funhouse is real. If you can do that, the illusions will have less of an effect on you. According to most Buddhists, thinking that you have a self is one of the funhouse illusions.[26] Our attachments and aversions originate from this illusion: we have hopes and fears because we care about ourselves. But, for the Buddhists, none of this is as it seems. Our so-called selves are just collections of fleeting physical and mental happenings— what the Buddhists sometimes call "aggregates."[27] Here is how Nāgārjuna, the Buddhist philosopher who lived between 150 and 250 AD, describes it in the *Rātnavalī* ("Precious Garland"): "The mental and physical aggregates arise/ From the conception of I which is false in fact/ How could what is grown/ From a false seed be true?"[28] The idea that you are a self keeps you imprisoned in the funhouse.

For most Buddhists, negative emotions are one of the classic symptoms of someone who is under the delusion of a self. Suppose I'm angry because my least favorite coworker made a snide comment to me. The reason I'm angry is because I feel insulted, but the Buddhists would say that there is no self to be insulted. According to Buddhism, I'm creating my own suffering by buying into the idea that I'm a self in the first place. Of course, the Buddhists have plenty of strategies to help you get over your bad feelings. Nāgārjuna advises you to consider "the harm others do you/ As created by your former deeds."[29] In other words, I should imagine that my least favorite coworker is my punishment for something I did in my previous incarnation. Not only does this stop me from constantly casting him as my enemy, it helps remind me that I need to stop the cycle of suffering by letting go of my anger. Strategies like these help us work our way into the idea that there is no self. Once we fully realize that, our negative emotions will go away.

While other philosophers may not think that the self is an illusion, they still think it's an obstacle to living well.[30] Iris Murdoch, the 20th-century English philosopher, is one example. She thinks that one of the central aspects of a good life is being able to free yourself from your own self-centered fantasies. For Murdoch, one of the main aims of philosophy is to figure out how to "defeat the fat relentless ego."[31] Reflecting on a good life should lead us to direct our attention away from ourselves. As Murdoch puts it, "when clear vision has been achieved, self is a correspondingly smaller and less interesting object."[32] The less self-concern we have, the more open we will be to the good things in life—community, compassion, and love. The person living the best life is one who doesn't think much about the self at all.

But the connection between caring less about yourself and greater feelings of community isn't as straightforward as the Buddhists make it out to be. Remember the problem that Latimer from George Eliot's *The Lifted Veil* poses for the Controlled Emotions Saints: he knows all the truths of the universe, but it doesn't bring him peace of mind. Instead, he's distant and oblivious to the people around him. Imagine a Buddhist version of Latimer.[33] Buddhist Latimer realizes that his self is an illusion. He sees his existence as impermanent and becomes less attached to his own life. Eventually, he starts to see all the concerns of his fellow humans in the same way. As long as they continue to be caught up in the illusion of themselves, he finds them tiresome. He thinks they are silly and small-minded, so he simply prefers to withdraw. He doesn't do this out of frustration or bitterness. He'd just rather not get entangled in their funhouse lives. Diminishing your self-love is supposed to make you more compassionate, but why wouldn't it be equally possible to become Buddhist Latimer? Caring less about yourself doesn't automatically lead you to care more about others. You might end up caring less about them.

The warnings against self-love and bad feelings both rest on the assumption that they are preventing you from truly loving other people. But we know this is wrong. We can love multiple people at the same time: I love my spouse and I also love my friends. I don't love them the same way, but the two loves don't compete. If I can love lots of people at the same time, why can't I love myself and others too? Also, when you think about why your life matters to you, often you'll think of things that aren't you at all. One of the things that probably matters to you is your relationships to others—you are your child's mother or your father's daughter. Being a mother or a daughter is part of what makes you who you are. Your life is meaningful to you because of the people in it. If bad feelings are part of your attachment to your life, they are also part of the attachment to the people who matter most to you. You don't stop loving your spouse when you get mad at them; usually, you're angry *because* you love them. I get mad at my husband for climbing up a rickety ladder to clean the gutters because he's being cavalier with his health and safety, something that matters a lot to me. If I didn't care, I wouldn't be mad. Sometimes we have troubled relationships with family members and we stay angry at them for a long time. It's common for people to tell you that you should get over this anger—it's doing you no good, you know this person won't change, and you need to move on. This is a way of saying, "You care too much." Maybe it's good advice: sometimes it's better not to stay in a relationship that's hurting you. But getting over your anger means emotionally detaching yourself from that person. Staying angry at someone can be a way of staying invested in the relationship. It may not feel good, but sometimes keeping the connection, even when it's an angry one, is better than cutting the line altogether. We often think that self-love and loving others pull us in two different directions, but that's not true. Caring about your life means caring about all the people who make your life meaningful. Bad feelings aren't preventing you from caring about people; you feel them because you care.

Self-love, like love for other people, can get distorted and obsessive. But that doesn't mean self-love is somehow inherently dangerous. Once we let go of that idea, there's no reason to think that we can't love other people and ourselves at the same time. And if self-love isn't as dangerous as we think, the bad feelings that go with it aren't so dangerous either. Skeptics will point out all the selfish, egotistical things people do with their bad feelings and try to convince you that most people love themselves too much. I'm not denying that people can be selfish and egoistic. But we have to figure out who the real troublemaker is. Often the real problem isn't too much self-love; it's the wrong kind. Building a self that's really yours and that you feel proud of is one of the hardest parts of being human. No one can live your life for you, but that means you have to make all the decisions yourself and there's no guidebook. We're all making it up as we go along and sometimes it seems like everyone else knows what they're doing. We're likely to be full of self-doubt, but we kid ourselves with feigned confidence. It's easy to react to this self-doubt by burying it in false bravado. What looks like too much self-love might be a paper-thin mask hiding the fear of not knowing or not liking who we are.

Selves aren't fat and relentless. They are fragile and unstable. To love one is to love something always half-formed and precarious. And it's hard to know how to love something like that. The real challenge we face is learning how to love it honestly—without apology but also without defensiveness. We have to embrace the half-formed, precarious thing exactly as it is. This kind of self-love is the key to living well with our bad feelings. One philosophy's best sinners can help us learn it.

The Old Immoralist

In 1844, Friedrich Nietzsche (pronounced "nee-tcha") was born in Röcken, a small village in a Prussian province.[34] His father died when Friedrich was 5 years old, and he was raised by his mother and his grandmother. He studied the classics—Greek and Latin poetry and classical languages. He became a university professor at the tender age of 24 but then served as a medic in the Franco-Prussian War (1870–1871). After contracting an illness during the war, Nietzsche struggled with health problems, which forced him into early retirement at 38. He spent the rest of his life as a nomad, traveling all over Europe and writing. Most of his works were published during his wandering years in the late 1870s until 1888. While he was in Italy in 1889, he suffered a mental and physical breakdown. He never regained his sanity and was left in the care of his mother and younger sister until he died in 1900.

Nietzsche is best known for quotations taken wildly out of context. People know he said things like "God is dead" and "What doesn't kill you makes you stronger," but they don't know what these words actually mean. Nietzsche's legacy was damaged significantly by his younger sister, Elisabeth. She collected and published some of his works after his death and put her own nationalist, anti-Semitic spin on them. Her ugly ideology was a source of tension with her brother: he nearly disowned her when she married Bernhard Förster, a rabid anti-Semite who wanted to establish a German colony in Paraguay.[35] Once Nietzsche lost his sanity, Elisabeth took over his estate, crafted him as a pro-Aryan jingoist, and exploited his name for money. After he died, she intentionally courted an association between Nietzsche and Nazi ideology: she constructed an archive of Nietzsche's works, and Hitler helped with the funding.[36] Nietzsche would have loathed all of this, but sadly Elisabeth's version of him is the one that many people know. To this day, Nietzsche is beloved by neo-Nazis, anti-Semites, and fascists—people he would have hated.

Nietzsche's work invites misunderstandings because it's cryptic, dramatic, and metaphorical. To get sense of his project, you need to read multiple works, understand his historical context, and know what his influences were. One of his inspirations was Montaigne, the Renaissance philosopher and author of the *Essays*, whom we met in the Introduction. Nietzsche loved Montaigne and was obsessed with what he called Montaigne's "cheerfulness."[37] One of the big themes in Montaigne's work is the imperfection of human nature. We make mistakes, we're inconsistent, we're weak-willed, and we're not as aware of our flaws as we should be. Montaigne accepts all this and yet doesn't despair: he loves life, himself, and his fellow humans despite the faults. Nietzsche marveled at this mindset. He wrote that Montaigne had a "cheerfulness that really cheers."[38] It wasn't a false cheerfulness that came from someone who "simply does not see the sufferings and the monsters he purports to see and combat," but rather the cheerfulness of "a victorious god with all the monsters he has combated."[39] Montaigne, in other words, wasn't naïve about people or life. He knew exactly how terrifying and maddening both could be, and yet he loved them anyway. Nietzsche wanted to figure out how we could all obtain something like Montaigne's honest cheerfulness, but he thought we face many obstacles. One of the biggest is inside your own head.

Nietzsche thinks our souls are very sick and that The Saint is to blame for the illness.[40] The Saint is a figure of Nietzsche's construction: think of it as a title that applies to anyone who adopts a pessimistic view of humans. It sounds surprising to say that a saint would be a pessimist, but Nietzsche's Saint is not a Mother Teresa type. While Montaigne embraces human imperfection with love and acceptance, The Saint responds with contempt and rejection. The Saint thinks people are corrupt: they are wicked, animalistic, and weak. Nietzsche describes this attitude as the "Christian distress of the mind that comes from sighing over one's inner depravity."[41] Nietzsche usually associates The Saint with early Christian philosophers, but the title is given to anyone who thinks the imperfection of human nature requires salvation. That salvation comes in many guises—God's grace, reason, science, or art. Whatever form it takes, the message is the same: following this thing is the only way to redeem yourself. Beg God for forgiveness, be as rational as possible, wed yourself to the objectivity of science, or follow the flights of artistic genius. Only then can you rise above your abysmal human flaws. Because The Saint thinks human beings are corrupt, he encourages you to treat yourself with suspicion. As Nietzsche puts it, he sees himself "as a battlefield upon which good and evil spirits wrestle."[42] According to The Saint, there are evil forces lurking inside you, and you have to maintain constant vigilance against them. Nietzsche thinks this attitude ends up fragmenting your psychology into pieces. In order for someone to worship "part of himself as God," he needs to "diabolize the other part."[43] You become a tyrant to yourself. What's truly sick about all this, according to Nietzsche, is that we start to enjoy the battle. We feel good about ourselves when we can defeat our inner demons. It makes us feel powerful and triumphant, and so we keep looking inside ourselves for more battles to fight. We become our own worst enemies.

Nietzsche thinks the fragmented psychology of The Saint is built on a lie. Human beings were never contemptible or corrupt to begin with. We never needed salvation because there was never anything wrong with us. What The Saint called corruption was just part of being a human who is fully alive in the world. Take selflessness as an example. The Saint will tell you that you have to be as selfless as possible; otherwise you are selfish and rotten. Nietzsche asks: "How could the ego act without an ego?"[44] If you didn't have a sense of self that you cared about, why would you ever act in the world at all?[45] You can see why Nietzsche disagreed with the Buddhists (they are also versions of The Saint). In order to accept that the self is an illusion, you have to convince yourself that your existence in the world as you know it is fake.[46] Nietzsche asks: how are you supposed to live like that? If we really started thinking of ourselves this way, we would just stop living. Nietzsche thinks that living a human life is inseparable from valuing, caring, or having things matter to you.[47] Being alive isn't just existing; it's *feeling* alive and having something to *live for*. For Nietzsche, the opposite of life isn't death. It's nihilism: when we stop valuing anything and everything seems meaningless.[48] We stop living when life stops mattering to us.

This is why Nietzsche thinks The Saint is dangerous. The Saint might deny it, but deep down he hates himself and he wants everyone else to hate themselves. But hating yourself is a direct threat to your life. The more you tear into yourself and try to kill your self-love, the less attached you are to living. If you don't matter to you anymore, Nietzsche thinks nothing will matter to you. And that road leads straight to nihilism. So, how do we stop all this and reverse course? Here's the bad news: we can't. The Saint has transformed our entire way of seeing ourselves and Nietzsche thinks we'll never be whole the way we used to be. The good news is that we can invent new ways to be. We might be sick now, but we can get better. Nietzsche has many ideas about how we can change, but one of the first steps is to stop being afraid of what's inside you. People have been telling you that you have a wild horse in you that needs to be broken. Nietzsche asks: what if the real problem is that you're holding the reins too tight?

The Lovely Human Beast

One of Nietzsche's favorite edicts is *amor fati*: Latin for "love of fate."[49] Loving fate means loving the entirety of your life and yourself—the good and the bad, the joyful and the painful, and everything in it that is "wild, arbitrary, fantastic, disorderly, and surprising."[50] Don't break your wild horse. Love it exactly as it is. *Amor fati* is the attitude we need to live well with our bad feelings.[51] First, it requires acceptance. Acceptance doesn't just mean you should stop fighting your negative emotions. When people talk about emotional management, they'll often say that you should admit what you're feeling because it does no good to deny it. Unfortunately, the next thing out of their mouths is usually some kind of advice about how to get rid of your bad feelings or replace them with better ones. Admitting your feelings is often seen as the first step in the process of eventually getting over them. But if there's nothing wrong with bad feelings, there's no reason to get rid of them. The acceptance of *amor fati* means realizing that negative emotions are valuable because they are expressions of your self-love and that your life would be meaningless without them. *Amor fati* also means having an attitude of loving curiosity toward your bad feelings.[52] As Nietzsche would put it, you need to have "a gentleness with what is strange."[53] Negative emotions can be frightening, confusing, surprising, and painful. Being gentle with them means being open to experiencing them even when we don't quite understand them or know how to handle them. Our attitude toward them should be exploratory rather than condemning. Instead of looking inside ourselves with suspicion, Nietzsche uses the analogy of an adventurer who sails around the coastline of his "inland sea"—not to conquer it but to discover it.[54] You have to be willing to let your emotions go where they want to go and to follow them rather than try to lead them. When bad feelings happen, just feel them.

We usually resist freeing our emotions because we're afraid that if we let ourselves feel them, we'll feel them forever, they'll consume us, or we'll hurt someone. Some of this fear comes from The Saint, who has convinced us that they represent something wicked inside us. There's nothing wicked about your attachment to your own life, and your negative emotions are just part of that attachment. Bad feelings are not going to eat you: you will feel them and then they will eventually go away. Some of the fear comes from seeing the damage that negative emotions can do. But the damage doesn't happen because of the feelings. It happens because of what we do to and with them. They become terrors because we make them that way. If we're going to avoid this outcome, we need to learn how to loosen up on the reins.

One of the strongest temptations we face when we experience a negative emotion is to *do something* with it. Imagine you find yourself envying your neighbor's new car. You might be tempted to try to get rid of your feeling as quickly as possible. One way to do that is to judge yourself harshly—envying your neighbor's car is immature or materialistic. You give yourself a quick chastisement to chase the feeling away. You might try to quickly divert your attention or try to focus on something positive. Chiding yourself or trying to immediately look on the bright side means you're not really listening to what your feelings are trying to tell you. It's a way of denying your feelings rather than admitting them. Sometimes we turn our bad feelings into something else, just like Satan does in *Paradise Lost*. You might convince yourself that your neighbor is being a showboat: look how he parked the shiny new car in his driveway rather than in his garage. He's clearly rubbing it in everyone's face. Now your envy transforms into righteous indignation about your neighbor's bad behavior. This isn't honest: you're not allowing your envy to just be what it is. Instead of turning your envy into a different feeling, you might instead find a way to talk yourself out of it. One common response to envy is "sour grapes." The term comes from Aesop's fable "The Fox and the Grapes." In the story, the fox tries and fails to reach the grapes on the vine, so he convinces himself that he doesn't really want them because they're probably sour. So, you convince yourself that your neighbor's car isn't that great after all. Maybe you tell yourself you're not the sort of person who cares about cars anyway or that you're trying to consume less because you care about the planet. You try to convince yourself that you actually prefer the clunker sedan sitting in your own driveway. Your leather seats are already broken in and you wouldn't like the stiffness of new leather. Just like looking on the bright side, this is another way of denying what you feel.

Doing things with our feelings is one of the most common traps we fall into, and it's one of the places where trouble starts. Why are we so prone to it? One reason is the bad reputation bad feelings have. If you've been told all your life that negative emotions are dangerous and pathological, you're probably convinced that there's something wrong with you when you feel them. If you believe that bad feelings are like drugs and you can get addicted to them, you want to snuff them out before they take over. Another reason is that they are sometimes painful. Unlike joy, for instance, anger or envy doesn't always feel good to feel. Emotional hygiene advocates are happy to point out that being angry takes work and energy. Sometimes people want to get over their negative emotions not for any high-minded reason, but just because they're tired of feeling them.

There's also a deeper reason: bad feelings make us feel vulnerable. You envy your neighbor's car because you want something like it in your own life. Maybe it's not just the car, but the kind of success or financial freedom the car represents. Your envy tells you: I don't have what I want in my life, I am lacking something, or my life doesn't look how I want it to look. Admitting you feel envy requires you to own up to a feeling of incompleteness or loss. Not only that, but we don't choose to have our bad feelings—or our good feelings, for that matter. We don't have direct control over any of our emotions, but we tend to be less embarrassed by and suspicious of the positive ones. You usually don't feel vulnerable if you're "caught" feeling joy. Negative emotions are unwelcome because they show up when we don't feel good about ourselves. Here comes envy, uninvited and speaking your hurt. And if the rumors about bad feelings are true, your envy is evidence of flaws like shallowness or immaturity. Now you've failed twice: once in lacking what your neighbor has and once in feeling envy about it in the first place. We are unwilling to own up to our bad feelings because we judge ourselves for feeling them and because we think others are likely to judge us as well. Bad feelings also force your self-love straight to the surface, and you're supposed to be embarrassed about that too. Admitting you feel envy means admitting your self-love right along with it—I'm envious because I'm lacking something in *my* life. If you believe that self-love is selfish, your envy has now betrayed you as an immature, self-absorbed loser with clunker sedan.

None of this feels good, so instead of just sitting there and feeling bad, we rush to do something with our envy—chase it away, bury it, turn it into a righteous crusade, or use it as motivation for self-improvement. But there's another option. We could just feel it. Next time you feel envy, try just saying it aloud without saying anything else: "I'm envious of the neighbor's car." Say it and then stop—no explanation and no chastisement. If hearing the words makes you squirm, resist the urge to console yourself, beat yourself up, or talk yourself out of the feeling. Just sit with it and let yourself feel what you feel, even if it's painful or uncomfortable. We resist this because we're afraid that we won't be able to control our feelings. But what if we just accepted that we don't control them? Deep down you already know this—you can't make yourself feel something you don't, and you can't turn your feelings off like a faucet. Yet your inner tyrant seems to insist on having a stranglehold on everything inside you—everything must be under control all the time. This is holding the reins too tight. What if you just accepted that your emotional life can be unpredictable? Sometimes you'll be surprised, confused, and even embarrassed about your feelings. There's no reason to be concerned when your feelings don't do what you want or expect; that's just how emotions are.

We think we have to control our negative emotions because if we let them loose, they'll torch everything in our lives. It's like being possessed by a demon: envy will take over your mind and you'll suddenly find yourself smashing the windshield of the neighbor's new car with a baseball bat. Notice that the emotion double standard has appeared again—no one ever gets worried about being possessed with gratitude. Do people use their bad feelings as a reason to hurt other people? Absolutely, but it's not because they're possessed. Lashing out is a way we cope with the fact that negative emotions feel bad; it's a way of refusing to just feel them. I don't want to just sit there and let my envy speak my hurt and tell me I don't have what I want in my life. So instead, I'll grab the baseball bat from my garage and start swinging. Lashing out like this feels automatic because we often do it quickly, but that doesn't mean the emotions have taken over your mind. It just means we're quick to try to dodge the pain bad feelings bring rather than just experience it. We do hurtful and destructive things because we don't like what our bad feelings are telling us. They show up when our sense of self feels shaky. Sometimes they arrive to defend our sense of self: we get angry when people insult or mistreat us. Sometimes, like envy, they're telling us we're not who we'd like to be. Bad feelings come around when we're feeling vulnerable and powerless. Doing something vindictive, hurtful, and destructive makes us feel better because it makes us feel powerful. If I'm swinging the baseball bat, I'm the one in charge now.[55] It gives me something to do rather than just sit there and feel like a loser. Because people tend to respond to bad feelings in unhealthy and immature ways, we tend to think the emotions themselves are unhealthy and immature. But we're the ones causing the trouble and pinning the blame on our feelings. They make an easy scapegoat because they already have a bad reputation. In reality, we do bad things with our feelings because we don't know how to just let ourselves feel bad.

Learning how to be honest about what you're feeling and letting yourself feel it without doing anything else are key to living well with negative emotions, but they aren't easy to do. Admitting what we're feeling can be challenging because often we have a hard time figuring out what we feel. Emotions don't always come to us clearly labeled, and we sometimes need help figuring out how to name the experience. We should take a cue from Darwin: pay attention to your emotions.[56] Notice what they feel like and try to describe them. Compare them to your other emotions. Enlist the help of a friend or loved one to talk through it with you. Like Darwin, be open to the idea that negative emotions are intelligent. Bad feelings are part of our attachment to our lives: they help us discover what we care about and they express what we care about. We'd be lost without them.

Once you've admitted what you feel, think about why you might be feeling it. What is it telling you about what matters to you? The easiest way to answer this question is to articulate the reasons why you feel what you feel—honestly and without getting defensive.

Maybe you envy your neighbor's car because nice cars represent success to you. Your envy is telling you that you haven't achieved the level of success you want, and that's a painful realization. Now, what should you do about this painful realization that envy is helping you have? Here are some traditional answers: you could resolve to change your situation—you can save more money or work more hours so that you can afford the nice car. Maybe you could reevaluate your definition of success so that the nice car plays a smaller role in the picture of your ideal life. You can do either of these, or you could take a different approach: do nothing. You are under no obligation to do anything with your painful realization or your envy. You don't have to use your envy as motivation, and you don't have to rearrange your priorities just because you feel it. You are a human being who is invested in your life, and that's good—you should care about you. Right now, your life doesn't look the way you want it to; your envy is telling you that, and it hurts. So, just let it hurt. All the pain is doing is telling you that you care about your life. Sometimes the only thing to do is live the pain.

In addition to lashing out and trying to shoo our feelings away, we also rush to justify our emotions by convincing ourselves that they represent some higher cause. Suppose I'm angry at my least favorite coworker because he corrected me in a meeting. It turns out he was right and I was wrong, but I'm still angry. Maybe I'm angry because he made me feel stupid. I might feel that way no matter who corrected me, but it stings more coming from my least favorite coworker (no one likes it when their least favorite person is right). There's no problem with my anger: it's just telling me that I felt insulted. But instead of just admitting that my least favorite coworker made me feel stupid and I didn't like it, I start building a case for my anger. I start thinking that he was trying to undermine me in front of the boss and he's out to wreck my career. I tell myself that he's an abuser or a bully. Now my anger isn't just my feeling anymore; it's my righteous stand against the enemy. I make myself the hero or the victim of the story and I use my anger to support that image of myself. I make my case to other people and try to convince them that they should also see him as a villain. Every slight or snub now becomes evidence of villainy, and every act of villainy becomes a target for my righteous anger.

If my bad feelings are about the villains out to get me, then they're not just about me anymore. Satan would never have convinced the other angels to go to war alongside him if he'd just been honest and said that he wanted to be God's favorite. Once he turns his jealousy into a beautiful speech about freedom and equality, the other angels take up arms. But justifying our bad feelings is often just another way of refusing to feel them. Why should we have to justify them at all? Why is it not OK for me to just feel bad without making my feelings someone else's fault? We feel compelled to justify our emotions because we don't think they're good enough as they are. We think they reflect badly on us, so we try to explain them away. Instead of just being part of our attachment to ourselves, we think they have to serve some higher cause. Loving your bad feelings means you have to love them honestly, and turning them into righteous justifications isn't honest. You're not letting them speak their language; you're making them say what you want them to say. If you can learn to sit with the bad feeling, you don't need to go looking for justifications for it—and you won't have to live in a world surrounded by enemies of your own invention.

Often when we try to justify our feelings this way, we're trying to make our sense of self feel more stable and secure. If my least favorite coworker is the villain and I'm the hero, I have a clear role to play and I get to be the good guy. I get to imagine myself persevering and ultimately defeating my coworker in my quest for professional greatness—I can't let the haters win. It feels better to be a hero battling the enemy than to just accept the fact that I felt stupid and insulted. I can also paint myself as the innocent victim. Now I get to tell myself that everything that goes wrong in my life is due to my least favorite coworker's villainy. The victim role is comforting in a different way: if a villain controls my life, then I'm not responsible for anything that goes wrong. It's all my coworker's fault. This is how negative emotions turn into character traits and produce angry or envious people. My anger will keep coming to my defense as long as I keep telling myself that my coworker is the villain. People talk about "feeding" negative emotions, but it's not the emotions doing the eating. We feed anger to our fragile sense of self in the hopes that it will get bigger and stronger. When we see angry or envious people, we're not looking at someone who has been eaten up by an emotion. We're looking at someone who is using an emotion to hold themselves together. The problem is that they don't know how to let themselves fall apart.

Bad feelings cause the most trouble when we tyrannize them and refuse to just let them be what they are. Your bad feelings are expressions of your self-love, and they are in your life because you care about yourself. When they show up, it's usually because your sense of self gets bruised—you feel insulted, you feel betrayed, or you feel like a loser. And you won't be indifferent when something you love gets wounded. You might be tempted to think that this is the solution to getting rid of negative emotions: if I can just make my sense of self solid so that it never gets hurt, I won't feel them anymore. But that's not how lives and selves work. Your life changes in ways you can't anticipate, and your sense of who you are changes with it. When the tragedies and ecstasies of life come crashing in—the death of a loved one, a life-changing illness, falling in love, having a child—selves get blown apart and we have to remake them. Your sense of who you are is always fluid. Sometimes it feels relatively stable, and sometimes it feels like a house of cards. We have no reason to despair about this. It's *better* that your sense of self is a little precarious. If you spend most of your life trying to make sure that you always know exactly who you are, you might never question whether you're on the right track or discover some new possibility for yourself. You have to learn and relearn who you are over the course of your entire life. Loving a self honestly means accepting that it's fragile. And when it feels fragile, bad feelings will be there.

Your bad feelings are in your life because you care about it, and that's exactly how it should be. Trying to get rid of them or pushing them away is a mistake—you need them. Life is meaningful because they are in it. Your attachment to your life is one of the most important parts of a garden: the dirt. If the dirt isn't rich enough, nothing will grow. And good dirt is full of worms.

PART II

THE WORMS

"He that desires of a man to be made an angel, does nothing for himself"

Montaigne, "A Custom of the Isle of Cea"

"It does not speak against the ripeness of a spirit that it contains worms."

Nietzsche, *Human, All too Human*

4

Anger

Klu Klux Klan activity was on the rise in America in 1926, prompting W. E. B. Du Bois to write "The Shape of Fear." At the time, people responded to the Klan by "laughing it off," mocking Klan members who paraded around in "sheets and pillowcases."[1] But Du Bois points out that ridicule hadn't succeeded in getting rid of the Klan. The Klan was everywhere—not just in the American South, but also in Ohio, Colorado, Michigan, and New Jersey.[2] What was the cause of all this hate? According to Du Bois, hate begins in fear. Behind the "cruel-eyed demons who break, destroy, maim and lynch and burn at the stake is a knot, large or small, of normal human beings and these human beings at heart are desperately afraid of something."[3] Du Bois thinks we won't solve the problem of the Klan until we come to grips with the very human fear that lies behind its inhuman rage.

Our strategy for dealing with the kind of anger the Klan represents hasn't improved much since Du Bois's day. We still sometimes try to laugh it off, even when it's not wearing a sheet, but mockery isn't any more successful now than it was in 1926. Ridicule distances the Klan from us—they are ignorant, backward people playing dress-up in the woods. But ridicule obscures a terrifying fact: the Klan, as Du Bois points out, is doing a job "that the American people, or a considerable portion of them, want done."[4] Ninety-one years later in 2017, a torch-wielding white supremacist mob gathered in Charlottesville, Virginia, at the Unite the Right rally with not a sheet in sight. If there's a knot of normal humans at the heart of every mob, there's normal human anger at the heart of every twisted, hateful worldview. Does anger cause someone to pick up a torch or don a hood? Or is anger an unwilling accomplice in its own corruption? Philosophers have long been divided on the badness of anger. Some of them argue that anger is one of our worst emotions, and two of the most famous of these philosophers are Seneca and Śāntideva.

The Pestilence

Seneca was born sometime between 1 and 4 BC in Corduba, Spain.[5] He was involved in Roman politics but hardly had an easy career. He managed to survive serving under the notorious Emperor Caligula only to be exiled once Emperor Claudius took power. He was eventually called back to Rome to serve as a tutor to Claudius's stepson, Nero. Once Nero became emperor, Seneca tried his best to keep the young ruler in check. He managed it for a while, but things started to unravel after Nero poisoned his own mother. Seneca tried to retire from his position, but Nero wouldn't allow it. An assassination plot against Nero was uncovered, and Seneca's nephew Lucan was found to have been involved. Nero decided to punish his former tutor for it: he ordered Seneca to commit suicide in 65 AD.

Seneca spent a lot of time around angry people, so it's unsurprising that one of his major works, *De Ira* ("On Anger"), tackles the subject. Seneca minces no words when he describes just how bad anger is. In the opening lines of the essay, he writes: "Raging with an inhuman desire to inflict pain in combat and shed blood in punishment, it cares nothing for itself provided it can harm the other."[6] He calls it a "madness" that is "disfiguring" to the person who experiences it.[7] Seneca is clear that "no pestilence has been more costly for the human race."[8]

Seneca was a Stoic, and like his fellow Stoics whom we met in Chapter 1, he thinks we have a responsibility to eradicate anger. He agrees with Aristotle's definition of anger: it's a desire to hurt people who hurt us.[9] While Aristotle thinks anger can be appropriate,

Seneca argues that anger goes against our true nature. Human beings are social and seek affection from others. Anger goes against this tendency: it can cause us to "assault even the nearest and dearest."[10] Nothing good comes from it, it's always bad, and we'd be better off without it.

Seneca answers all the objections he thinks people will make to his anger prohibition. Aren't harsh words sometimes called for? Of course, people need to be corrected when they misbehave, but we should be stern and firm without yelling and screaming.[11] But why isn't mild anger acceptable? If your anger is really mild, it's because reason is in charge and is doing all the work.[12] If that's true, your anger is a pointless afterthought and you don't need it. Come on, Seneca, aren't we supposed to be angry at the enemy on the battlefield? Wrong again: anger makes us vulnerable to attack because it makes us careless.[13] But surely we should be angry at the people who harm our loved ones? Your devotion to your loved ones is motivation enough for you to protect them. Of course, many people do indeed get angry at those who harm their families, but people also get angry when "their hot bath is not properly prepared, if a glass gets broken, if their shoe is spattered with mud."[14] Seneca thinks there's nothing inherently righteous about anger. The anger you have toward the person who hurts your loved one is like the proverbial broken clock that's right twice a day. It's an accident that your anger is aimed at something that *seems* like a righteous cause.

Seven centuries later, Śāntideva (pronounced "shahn-ti-day-va") presented the Buddhist case against anger in the *Bodhicaryāvatāra* ("Guide to the Bodhisattva Way of Life"). Details of Śāntideva's life are hard to come by.[15] A couple of sources tell us that he was born into a royal family. The night before he was to take his place on the throne, divine personifications of Wisdom and Compassion appeared to him in a dream and told him not to become ruler. He fled into the wilderness and devoted himself to meditation. Śāntideva joined a Buddhist monastery, but his fellow monks thought he was a good-for-nothing. They demanded that he do a public recitation of a *sūtra* (a Buddhist religious text), thinking he would fail. According to one of his biographers, Śāntideva started to recite the *Bodhicaryāvatāra*, and when he got to a certain line in the text, he rose up into the sky and disappeared (though apparently his voice continued to recite the text).[16] Śāntideva turned up in another city and the monks from his monastery tried to get him to return, but he refused. He left monastic life and wandered India until he died.

Śāntideva is a Buddhist in the Mahāyāna tradition, which aims to develop *bodhicitta*, usually translated as the "awakened" or "enlightened" mind. Becoming *bodhicitta* means that you try to help all other sentient beings free themselves from suffering.[17] Central to achieving *bodhicitta* is the need to rid yourself of your mental afflictions—your cravings and aversions that arise from the illusion of the self. Only after you "liberate your fearing heart" can you help others.[18] Of course, one of the biggest mental afflictions is anger, which Śāntideva likens to a fire that will consume us unless we deprive it of fuel.[19] This is an image of anger we still use, all these centuries later.

Śāntideva thinks anger is pointless because it relies on a mistaken view about how the world really works. Using a medical analogy, he points out that when too much bile in the body causes pain, we're not angry at the bile. Bile isn't *trying* to hurt us. He then asks, "Why be angry at sentient beings, who are also provoked to anger by conditions?"[20] We get mad at people because we think they insult or harm us intentionally, but really people are just aggregates of mental and physical happenings—there's no difference between suffering caused by bile and suffering caused by my least favorite co-worker. If you see someone doing wrong, your response should be "Such are his conditions."[21] You should remind yourself that your bodily existence is impermanent, and someone who harms you physically is hurting a nonthing.[22] Someone who tries to wound you with words is likewise foolish because the mind is immaterial and can't be harmed.[23] Śāntideva thinks adopting these strategies will calm your anger and make you feel at ease.

For both Seneca and Śāntideva, anger is fundamentally irrational. It's based on false beliefs and is pointless or destructive. There's no right way or right time to feel it. Anger makes monsters or fools of us all.

The Protest

Given what Aristotle and Confucius say about anger, you can imagine they would disagree with Seneca and Śāntideva. Not only can anger be rational, but sometimes you *ought* to be angry, they would say. Feminist philosophers see a similar value in anger. Feminist philosophy, like Buddhism, is a complex tradition with many different voices. People associate feminism with the women's liberation movement in the United States during the 1960s–1970s, but feminist philosophy has been around much longer. The medieval Italian philosopher Christine de Pizan wrote a defense of women as far back as 1405 AD. In every time and place where philosophy happens, women have been doing philosophy and arguing for their right to be taken seriously.

Two influential defenses of anger appeared in the 1980s in the work of American feminists Marilyn Frye and Audre Lorde.[24] They focused on anger because women's anger is so often dismissed. When women get angry, they are told they are "acting crazy" or that they need to "calm down." Like Aristotle, Frye argued that you feel anger when someone mistreats you. More specifically, anger arises when you see that mistreatment as "unjust or unfair, or when you see it as due to someone's malice or inexcusable incompetence."[25] Anger is an emotion of protest—my anger is a way of saying that I matter and that no one has the right to meddle in my life without cause. When angry women are dismissed as "crazy," it's a refusal to hear their protests and a denial of their right to be free from interference.[26]

It's not just men who dismiss anger: White women are prone to dismiss Black women's anger as "crazy."[27] Audre Lorde's essay speaks directly to this issue. Living with racism day in and day out made her angry: "I have lived with that anger, ignoring, feeding upon it, learning to use it before it laid my visions to waste."[28] Despite anger's constant presence in her life, Lorde was not afraid of it. In fact, she thought learning to express her anger had given her a chance to grow.[29] The "well-stocked arsenal of rage" that all women possess can be "focused with precision" as a powerful kind of energy.[30] While some people see living with anger as a problem, Lorde thought the bigger problem was that we are afraid to speak our anger. Unspoken anger gets misused and misdirected. Women rarely learn how to be angry in healthy ways. Lorde admitted that "it is very difficult to stand and listen to another woman's voice de-lineate an agony I do not share, or to which I have contributed."[31] Like Frye, Lorde thought anger had truths to tell. As she put it, "when we turn from anger, we turn from insight."[32]

Contrary to Seneca and Śāntideva, Frye and Lorde consider anger to be a friend, not an enemy. Feeling and expressing anger is a way of standing up for ourselves, so we have no reason to be afraid of it. We'd be better off embracing it and learning to commu-nicate it.

The Good, the Bad, and the Boring

Seneca and Śāntideva paint a portrait of anger red in tooth and claw, bent on destruction. Frye and Lorde paint a portrait of anger standing defiant against those who want a boot on our necks. Which portrait captures the real anger? The Cultivated Emotions Saints can offer you a way out of the choice: both portraits are real. There's a good and a bad kind of anger. The bloody portrait is uncultivated, improper, out-of-control anger; the righteous one is cultivated, proper, harnessed anger. Living well with anger means we should feel the good kind and avoid the bad kind. As long as we're angry at the right things and in the right way, anger can be an important part of our lives.

What makes the bad kind of anger bad? The answer that probably comes to mind first is that anger is bad when we feel too much of it. Of course, Confucius and Aristotle think that too little anger is bad as well, but in everyday life we are usually less worried about people who don't feel enough anger. People are afraid of anger because they are sure that angry people hurt others and themselves. I've argued that too much anger is likely not what makes someone an angry person. Angry people have other problems—an insecure sense of self, unacknowledged hurt, or feelings of failure—and they're using anger to hold themselves together. That's not to deny that we sometimes lash out when we're angry. Lashing out is a coping mechanism that the philosopher Owen Flanagan calls "pain-passing." When we pass pain, we take our anger and say: "I am hurting, anxious, depressed, fearful, and wounded, and I strike out at you in anger and hurt you."[33] Lorde is right that women haven't learned (or been encouraged to learn) how to express and feel their anger well. I think this is true of most people. We're too quick to do things with our anger, we rush to talk ourselves into or out of it, and we often think expressing it amounts to just punching something or someone. We're particularly bad at just sitting with our anger and exploring it honestly. None of this is a problem with anger. What we do and don't do with our anger is the real problem.

The bad kind of anger isn't just about feeling too much of it. It's also about whether we're angry at the right things. Seneca and Śāntideva are happy to point out that most anger is trivial. I get mad when people call my favorite novel overrated, when someone in line ahead of me in the coffee shop takes forever to order, and when I have to spend hours on the phone with my insurance company. I'm usually not incandescent with rage (it depends on how long I've waited for the coffee), but I'm still angry. You might be tempted to say that I *shouldn't* be angry at things like the coffee shop line. It's not worth getting angry about—no one is hurting me, so what's the big deal? I shouldn't waste my energy.

Telling someone not to "waste their energy" is a way of advising them to have perspective. We shouldn't fly off the handle at every minor inconvenience, but having perspective doesn't mean I shouldn't be mad at the coffee shop line. The idea that we ought to float through life's little irritations without registering them at all is a denial of emotional reality. Think about Seneca's example of the broken glass. Suppose it's a glass you bought on one of your favorite vacations. While your kids are horsing around the house, they carelessly knock it off the shelf. Now one of your vacation memories lies shattered on the floor. A glass may not be important in the grand scheme of things, but we don't live our normal lives in the grand scheme of things. People are fond of telling you to look at the big picture when you're upset about something small. This is the same sort of reminder that Śāntideva would give you: next time someone takes a swing at you, remember that your physical existence is impermanent. In the *truly* grand scheme of things, broken glasses aren't important, but neither are you—human lives are tiny blips on the universe's radar screen. Looking at your life from that perspective is supposed to make all your cares and concerns seem small, but that's asking you to minimize your attachment to your life. Your cares and concerns matter to you because they're *yours*, even if they're small.

The idea that anger is good when it's about the right things presumes that somewhere there is a master list of things that are worth getting mad about it. We often argue over who has "the right" to be angry and who doesn't, and we tend to think that you're only allowed to be angry if you have good reasons for it. There are plenty of reasons to think we're not very good at making these judgments. The philosopher Myisha Cherry points out that White Americans often read the anger of Black Americans as excessive even when they have good reasons to be angry.[34] As Frye argues, men tend to think women's anger is always excessive and irrational. Notice also that the emotion double standard reappears here: no one tells you that you can only feel joy if you have good reasons. You're supposed to find joy in "the little things," but you can't be angry about them. Of course, people can be angry for bad reasons, but often the real target of our criticism is the reasons rather than the feeling. If I have the expectation that I should never under any circumstances have to wait for coffee, that's a bad reason to get angry, but it's also a bad reason to feel confused, sad, or disappointed. Bad reasons are bad reasons, regardless of what feeling goes with them.

Figuring out who has good or bad reasons for anger is harder than it looks. Emotional criticism can quickly turn into emotional policing.[35] Emotional police tend to use overly narrow criteria in judging a feeling appropriate or rational. Fear of flying is a good example: people swoop in and tell the person who is afraid of flying that there's nothing to fear. They cite statistics about the rarity of plane crashes and rattle off plane safety protocols to prove that flying isn't dangerous. But people who are afraid of flying don't always think of it in precisely these terms.[36] If you're afraid of heights or claustrophobic, flying is scary even if the plane doesn't crash. People who police anger assume that the only good reason to be angry is if someone intentionally harms you or someone else in a serious way. If you're angry about anything short of that, you are told that you're irrational or overreacting.

Thinking about anger in this way treats it like a perception: I think I see a bird in the tree, but it's actually a squirrel. If I keep insisting it's a bird, I'm just wrong. My perception is correct when it matches the way the world is. Sometimes emotions work this way. I think my least favorite coworker slashed my tire, but really there's a nail in it. If I stay angry at him for something he didn't do, my anger is just wrong. But emotions don't always function exactly like perceptions. They don't just reflect the way the world is; they are part of how I experience the world.[37] I'm afraid of roller coasters because their speed and height scare me, but other people find them thrilling. It's not as though one of us has to be wrong. There's no fact of the matter about whether roller coasters are scary—there's no single correct way to experience them. Our experiences of the world are complex, and our emotions are often sensitive to more than one thing. If your kids break your favorite glass by accident, it's easy for someone to say you shouldn't be mad because they didn't mean to do it. But your anger might not be about whether they meant to break it. You might be angry because the broken glass makes you feel like you don't have any space of your own or that you can't display your favorite things without them getting ruined. Anger that looks like it doesn't have good reasons might be about something else that isn't obvious at first glance.

Most of the time we feel angry when we feel like we're being treated as though we don't matter. Frye described anger as "a claim that one is a being whose purposes and activities require and create a web of objects, spaces, attitudes, and interests that is worthy of respect."[38] Anger is the emotion of self-defense. When someone interferes with my life, I get angry because my life matters to me. Caring about my life means I want to protect it from threats like physical harm, but also from intrusion or insult. Those intrusions or insults don't have to be huge injustices. The people who are dithering in front of me at the coffee shop are keeping me from going on with my day. Are they doing me a grave wrong? Of course not, but my plans are still being interfered with. Because the line at the coffee shop pales in comparison to injustice, we conclude it's not worth being mad about. But the fact that it's less important doesn't mean it's not important at all. Anger can be about minor inconveniences as well as grave wrongs and everything in between. There's nothing wrong with getting mad about life's little irritations. You care about your life, including the boring and trivial parts of it.

The biggest problem we have with anger is that we tend to make it someone else's problem. Jumping to accuse other people of treading on us is a way of doing something with our anger. I turn my anger on the people in front of me at the coffee shop—it's their fault I have to wait. I can *feel* stepped on even if no one actually steps on me, but that doesn't make my anger mistaken. Like the broken glass, the fact that I feel mistreated might arise from something other than actual mistreatment. The solution isn't to try to "correct" my anger. I just need to be honest with myself about why I feel what I feel instead of assuming that someone must be to blame for making me feel this way.

Fight the Power

Philosophers often argue that anger is good when it's about injustice, unfairness, or major harms—what I'll call *righteous anger*.[39] When Frye and Lorde argued that anger is the right response to sexism and racism, they are defending righteous anger.[40] Some defenses of anger go one step further. Like the old bumper sticker that reads, "If you're not outraged, you're not paying attention," some people argue that we if we're not angry, it's because we're oblivious to terrible things going on in the world.[41] We should be angry and we should use our righteous anger in constructive ways—to correct wrongs and change things for the better.

People who defend righteous anger often believe it's a special kind of anger, unlike the mundane anger from the coffee shop.[42] Dividing anger into kinds is something philosophers love to do because it's supposed to help distinguish the good kind of anger from the bad kind. But if you reject the idea that there is "bad anger," there's no reason to carve our emotions up into different kinds. We feel anger about many different things, but that doesn't mean each object has its own emotion. There's no "broken glass anger" or "coffee shop anger" or "injustice anger." There's just anger and what we make of it. Emotions, like colors, can have different shades and tones. Scarlet, garnet, and vermillion are all shades of red, even though they look different from each other. Anger can be tinged with bitterness, fear, or shame. It can also range from unbridled rage to niggling irritation. But there's just one feeling, and we feel it about a variety of things and in a variety of strengths. Anger over a broken glass is not a different emotion from anger over slashed tires. Of course, the two don't feel quite the same. Vermillion and garnet don't quite look the same either, but they're both red. Our goal shouldn't be to try to only feel the right kind of anger. Our goal should be to learn how to feel all our anger honestly.

Defending righteous anger as the only good anger has downsides. People are fond of telling you that you should use your anger constructively to fight injustice, but this treats emotions as valuable only if they're productive. It implies that anger is destructive and that it will eat you up from the inside unless you "channel" it into something constructive. The idea that only righteous anger is good also feeds our tendency to rewrite our anger into a story about injustice even when it isn't. I tell myself that when my least favorite coworker corrects me, he's trying to ruin my career instead of just accepting that I'm angry because he made me feel stupid. We're more apt to try to marshal other people into our anger if we think it's righteous. Not only do I tell myself that my coworker is a villain, I also try to convince other people that he's a villain.

Demanding that anger be righteous forces it into the service of, as James Baldwin put it, "the good of society."[43] Baldwin makes this complaint about certain types of novels, like Harriett Beecher Stowe's *Uncle Tom's Cabin* and Richard Wright's *Native Son*, that try to serve the cause of combating racism (albeit in different ways).[44] Baldwin objects that so-called protest novels don't treat their characters as human beings; they are merely representatives of their "societal realities."[45] The failure of these novels lies in their "rejection of life, the human being, the denial of his beauty, dread, power."[46] When art is made to serve noble causes rather than tell a human story, Baldwin thinks it ends up portraying complex human beings as oversimplified caricatures. I think righteous anger does something similar.[47] Righteous anger is the emotional equivalent of a comic book hero; it exists only to fight the bad guys. Righteous anger can't really be mine anymore—I'm supposed to feel it only on other people's behalf. If I do feel anger on my own behalf, it has to be because I'm the victim of a serious wrong. I can't, for example, be mad at my spouse for not unloading the dishwasher unless I turn not unloading the dishwasher into some kind of violated obligation. I get to care about myself only as a victim of injustice and not as a human with a life. Only allowing yourself to feel righteous anger shrinks the messy, complex human part of yourself.

I'm not arguing that we shouldn't be angry about injustice, but anger about injustice isn't a special or noble kind of anger. We feel angry because we care about our lives. If someone puts a boot on our neck, they're saying we don't matter—why *wouldn't* we be angry about that? We also care about the lives of others. Our lives are meaningful partly because of the connections we have to other people. Those connections don't just involve the people who are close to us. We see a fellow human with a boot on their neck and our anger protests it in the same way we protest a boot on our own neck. But this doesn't have to be a special kind of anger. Defenders of righteous anger often think we *ought* to be angry at injustice—if we aren't, we're not really paying attention, like the bumper sticker says. But we know our emotions don't automatically follow our judgments. We don't decide to feel angry just because we think we ought to or expect to. You might see something as a terrible injustice and, perhaps to your own surprise, not feel angry. Maybe you're utterly horrified, profoundly sad, completely disgusted, or just numb. Emotions that look nontraditional aren't necessarily wrong—remember Du Bois's grief for his baby son. If you responded to injustice with a shrug, we might think you don't appreciate the gravity of the situation or that you're heartless. We want people to be moved when they see injustice happening because we want them to care about it, but there's no reason to think that anger is the only way to care about something.

Defending anger only when it's righteous isn't really defending it at all. We're only willing to defend it when it's Lowly Worm, all cleaned up and making itself useful. We feel anger for the same reason we feel other negative emotions: we're attached to ourselves and our lives. I'm angry when I feel mistreated, and I'm angry when people I care about—including people I don't know—are mistreated. I also get mad when people take too long ordering coffee and when someone gives my spouse's fiction a bad review. We don't have to save our anger only for grave wrongs. Being angry is part of how we care about our lives, and our lives are made up of both big and small concerns.

The Outrage Machine

There's no shortage of anger on the internet. People take to social media to write passionate condemnations of injustice as well as hateful screeds. We fight with strangers, old high school acquaintances, and family members in the comments section of a post. Internet outrage makes the strongest case that anger is addictive: we seem to log on every day just to get our fix. But anger isn't the culprit. When we scroll through social media, we see other people doing stupid and cruel things. We get angry at them, and we tell ourselves that we're better than they are. It's a cheap way to gain self-assurance: if I'm angry at the stupid and cruel people in the world, then I know I'm not one of them. Social media is attractive in part because of the technology involved: the algorithms prioritize posts that get more "engagement," so things that enflame and provoke are spread around.[48] It's also easy to access. We open our timelines with a simple click, and we can scroll mindlessly for hours through a parade of people we can judge. It makes us feel righteous, smart, and informed; we're paying attention, after all. So, we log on, get angry, and feel good about ourselves.

More than once, digital rage has crawled out of the screen. In May 2014, Elliot Rodger posted a video of himself on YouTube where he laid out his plans for what he called the "Day of Retribution." He would go to the Alpha Phi sorority of the University of California Santa Barbara and "slaughter every single spoiled, stuck-up, blonde slut I see inside there."[49] When he was unable to get into the sorority house, he shot at three women nearby, killing two and wounding one. He then drove around shooting at people from his car, killing one more person and injuring thirteen others before shooting himself.[50]

Rodger was an incel: a shorthand term for "involuntary celibate."[51] The first incel group was started by a woman in the 1990s as a way for people unlucky in love to help support each other through their loneliness. Today, incels are a subgroup of what is known as the "manosphere," a collection of loosely affiliated misogynist online groups. Incels bond over their lack of romantic and sexual experience. They've created their own lexicon that they use in their online forums. Attractive men who sleep with lots of women are called "Chads," and the women who sleep with them are "Stacys." Rodger has become a hero in the incel world: he is occasionally referred to as "Saint Elliot" or "the supreme gentleman" (a term he used for himself in the video). Some incels have developed elaborate conspiracy theories and pseudoscientific justifications for their worldview. Many believe, for example, that facial bone structure is correlated with attractiveness, so they do exercises (known as "mewing") to enhance their jawlines. They think women wrongly reject them and that their inability to "get girls" is unfair or unjust. For the majority of incels, the best solution to their problem is to take away women's rights to decide who to sleep with. To put it bluntly, they think women should be forced to have sex with them.

Incels are angry—angry at the way their lives have turned out, angry at men who are more attractive than they are, and angry at women who don't do their bidding. Maybe you think we should be more accepting of feelings of anger, but not *this* anger. I have no interest in defending incels, but as Du Bois argues, understanding violent ideologies requires understanding the normal human emotions at their core. We make monsters of our bad feelings because we refuse to let them be what they are. Monster-making is on full display in the incel world.

At some point in your life, you've probably felt rejected and unlovable. Everyone else seems to be successful while you're languishing on the sidelines. You lament the monotony of your life and feel trapped in a never-ending cycle of disappointment. You might be angry at the universe for giving you a raw deal, but it's hard to be angry at the universe: it has no face to spit in and it never answers back when you yell. Your anger has an uncomfortable nebulous feel, drifting to various targets but never really settling on anything or anyone for long. It hangs over your life like a fog.

You start looking for things to do with your anger instead of just experiencing the unpleasantness. You look for a scapegoat to pin it on, to give the nebulous feelings a definite shape. If your story has a villain, then someone is responsible. It's much easier to be a victim of someone else's villainy than it is to be unlucky. Being unlucky is arbitrary and random—it's just a roll of the dice. Finding a villain protects you from facing the possibility that life just isn't fair and that no one is ever promised success. You also don't have to entertain the thought that your misery might be the result of your flaws or bad choices. Self-examination is hard, sometimes painful, and people rarely learn how to do it well, if they learn how to do it at all. If you're the victim of someone else's wickedness, you can point to the villain as the cause of your downfall.

The line between a violent misogynist and a lonely guy is not as sharp as it might seem. Many incels struggle with mental health, depression, and difficult life circumstances while also saying hateful, violent, and disgusting things about women.[52] Their views are extreme, but it's a mistake to conclude that they all must be psychopaths. It's likewise false to paint them as just "regular guys" who have gotten tough breaks in life. The human mind is a complicated place, and it only takes a few wrong turns on the internet for regular people to get sucked into bizarre and hateful worldviews. The incel story is fairly common: a lonely, awkward guy has never had much luck with dating.[53] He's still a virgin or hasn't had a girlfriend in a very long time. He's been rejected—in fact or maybe only in his mind—by most women he's interested in. At some point, he stumbles into or seeks out an online forum of other disaffected men like himself. There, he is introduced to junk science about evolution and the "sexual marketplace" that seems to explain everything about his experience. He finally finds people who understand what he's going through and feels like he belongs. He becomes convinced that women are to blame for his loneliness. Women are evil and they deserve to be punished. Incel ideology allows a man to live in a world, as the writer Laura Bates puts it, where he is "an aggrieved martyr."[54]

It's easy to look at incels and think they have too much anger, but the real problem isn't their feelings. The problem is that they use those feelings to build and reinforce a hateful ideology. Instead of simply learning how to sit with and be vulnerable to their bad feelings, incels try to comfort themselves by turning women into nefarious plotters who deprive them of their rightful "property." As the philosopher Kate Manne points out, Rodger believed that women *owed* him affection and they were wrongly withholding it from him.[55] In his manifesto, he wrote that women "denied me a happy life, and in return I will take away all of their lives. It is only fair."[56] Rodger made women the villains in his story. They were unjust and unfair to him, and he thought he had every right to punish them. Of course, this is all a delusion—one that he and other incels construct to avoid facing reality. But emotions don't build ideologies. Anger didn't tell Rodger that women were villains in his victim story. He told himself that story so that he could justify his anger, and so he could avoid feeling vulnerable, lesser, and lonely.

Incels aren't owed anything—not women's bodies and not pity or sympathy from the rest of the world. But they're allowed to be angry that their lives didn't turn out how they wanted; anyone who cares about their lives would be. At the same time, no one has the right to massive self-deception just so they can avoid the pain and hard work of self-examination. We don't have the right to try to protect ourselves from our own bad feelings by building a fantasy world, and we certainly don't have the right to demand that other people take that fantasy world seriously. Unfortunately, this is how many people make monsters out of their anger. We'd much rather create enemies than face our feelings of failure, disorientation, or loneliness. Having enemies lets us hide from self-doubt.

Avoiding making monsters out of anger means we have to explore it honestly. Anger shows up when we feel mistreated, but that doesn't necessarily mean anyone is actually mistreating us. Imagine a different version of an incel who is willing to be honest with himself about his anger. Instead of looking for someone to blame it on, he just sits with his anger and asks himself why he feels it. He might realize that even though he's angry because his life didn't turn out how he expected, that doesn't mean women are to blame for it. Without listening to and being honest about his anger, he may not have come to these realizations. We often think that if people let themselves feel emotions that don't look appropriate or don't make sense, they'll "feed" the emotions. This assumes that negative emotions are addictive—keep feeling them and you'll only make them worse. But incels end up where they are because they rush to construct justifications for their anger, and villains to blame it on (women), instead of thinking about why they're angry and being honest about it. They feel angry and then immediately assume they have a right to be. Misogyny, junk science, and a desire to avoid feeling vulnerable give them more than enough material to build those justifications.

The anger at the heart of hateful ideologies is often a cover for something else: the fear of not knowing who you are. Du Bois thinks the fear behind the Klan is a fear that the world is no longer made for you and that you will lose your place in it. White Americans are afraid that "the American Negro, despite all precautions, may force himself into a place where he will enter Congress, storm Wall Street, and marry White women."[57] Of course, White Americans have no right to hoard the world for themselves, and the fight for racial justice isn't about storming Wall Street. But Du Bois thinks we have to acknowledge that this is indeed what the Klan and other White Americans are afraid of. Why are they afraid of it? If you define yourself as the superior to an inferior, what happens when the inferior is no longer inferior? Your sense of self is destroyed. Once you realize that this is your fear, Du Bois thinks you have two choices: you can examine and express your fear openly and honestly, or you can reach for something to protect yourself, which is usually force and violence.[58] We face the same choice with anger. Many of us would rather lose ourselves in an alternate version of reality than take a hard look in the mirror. Behaving this way is grotesque and childish, but anger isn't what is whispering the lies in our ear. We're telling the lies to ourselves.

Anger is one of the bad feelings that is hardest for us to sit with. When we feel mistreated, we're quick to jump to our own defense by lashing out or looking for enemies. Sometimes someone is really intruding into our lives and sometimes we just feel that way. If we don't learn how to explore our anger honestly, we'll have a hard time telling the difference. Being honest about your anger doesn't mean you're only allowed to feel the good kind of anger or that you always have to have the right reasons to feel it. We don't have to talk ourselves out of it or train it so that it always behaves. There's no good anger or bad anger. There's just anger. We can turn it into a tool to fight injustice or a weapon to destroy our enemies, or we could learn to just feel it.

5

Envy and Jealousy

Of all the negative emotions, jealousy and envy have the reputation as two of the most dangerous—so much so that they are often depicted as actual monsters.[1] As Shakespeare's Iago famously puts it in *Othello*, jealousy is the "green-eyed monster which doth mock the meat it feeds on."[2] Iago is, of course, the embodiment of envy and the foil to Othello, who is destroyed by his own jealousy. In the ancient Mediterranean, envy was portrayed as an evil eye—the Latin word for "to envy" is *invidere*, which literally translates as "to look at with hostile intent."[3] People would sometimes install mosaics at the entrance to their houses that were meant to keep the evil eye of envy at bay. One of the most famous is from the House of the Evil Eye, which now resides in the Hatay Museum in Turkey. It shows a giant eye being attacked by a trident, a sword, a raven, a scorpion, a centipede, a serpent, a dog, and a panther (one apparently can't be too careful in warding off envy).[4] Ovid, the famous Roman poet from the 1st century BC, described envy as an evil woman who lives in a cave surrounded by a thick, dark fog.[5] She has pale skin, crooked eyes, and moldy teeth, and venom drips from her tongue because she eats snakes.[6] In 1304, the Florentine artist Giotto di Bondone painted a fresco of envy in the Arena Chapel in Padua.[7] This version shows a woman with a snake coming out of her mouth biting her in her own forehead. She has horns, huge pointed ears, and is surrounded by a ring of fire.

People tend to be especially reluctant to confess their feelings of envy and jealousy—and no wonder, since we insist on turning them into a phantasmagoria.[8] Nobody wants to be looked at like they have moldy teeth and horns. But envy and jealousy are less like monsters and more like the venomous snakes they supposedly feed on. They are closer to you than you realize—in your garden, behind that tree stump, or under those leaves. We exaggerate their dangers and assume they're out to get us. If we could just learn to leave them alone and let them be, we'd be far less likely to get bitten.

No Free Love

In English (and in some other languages), the words "envy" and "jealousy" are synonyms, but philosophers have traditionally argued that they pick out different emotions.[9] To figure out which feeling we're talking about, it helps to ask: is the emotion mainly about a what or a who? We're envious of other people for *what* they have: a beautiful beach house, a stellar singing voice, or a prestigious award. We're jealous of other people because of *who* they're close to: your best friend's other friend, your spouse's attractive coworker, or your father's stepchildren. We will often say "I'm so jealous of your trip to Hawaii" when we really mean we're envious. Sometimes we treat jealousy as though it's a milder version of envy. You might hear people say, "I'm not envious, I'm just jealous." But both envy and jealousy come in degrees: you can be a little bit envious and very, very jealous. You can feel both emotions toward the same person. I might be jealous of my best friend's other friend and also envious of her gorgeous hair. Whether you think they're the same or not, both jealousy and envy have bad reputations.

Jealousy has been charged with being destructive or regressive or both. Shakespeare's Othello is one of the popular jealous characters in literature, but Medea, the title character from the 5th-century BC play by the Greek playwright Euripides, is a more vicious green-eyed monster.[10] Medea falls in love with the mythic hero Jason of the Argonauts. Being well versed in magic, she aids him repeatedly in his quest to obtain the Golden Fleece. She even betrays her father and kills her brother so she can escape her home country and sail to

Corinth to be with Jason. She bears Jason two sons. After everything she does for him, he leaves her to marry another (younger) woman who will enhance his political aspirations. Nearly 2000 years before the line "hell hath no fury like a woman scorned" was penned, Medea proclaims, "Woman on the whole is a timid thing . . .but wronged in love, there is no heart more murderous."[11] And murderous she is. Medea satisfies her jealous rage by avenging Jason's betrayal. She creates a poisonous dress and gives it to Jason's new bride as a gift. The dress burns the woman alive and also kills the bride's father who embraces her while she writhes in pain. Medea then takes what Jason cares for most: their children. She kills her sons, showing their bodies to Jason in her final speech before fleeing with them in a chariot. Jealous lovers outside of Greek tragedy are rarely so creative, but we still see them as dangerous. The trope of the jealous woman has endured far beyond Medea, from the movie *Fatal Attraction* to Alanis Morrisette's song "You Oughta Know." We think of jealousy as a particularly powerful emotion that takes over its possessor and drives them to hurt their rival and even the people they love.

When jealousy isn't dangerous, it's sometimes seen as backward or unenlightened. The philosopher Jerome Neu writes, "It was one of the hopes of the sixties (as of many other periods) that by restructuring social relations it might be possible to eliminate jealousy and other painful, 'bourgeois' passions."[12] Life in the Los Angeles area of Laurel Canyon seemed that way in the 1960s.[13] Laurel Canyon was once home to some of the era's most famous musicians: Frank Zappa, Joni Mitchell, Jim Morrison, Mickey Dolenz, Cass Elliott, and David Crosby, to name just a few. Johnny Echols, the lead guitarist for the band Love, likened Laurel Canyon to the fictional Land of Oz. It was a magical world set apart—a "bubble of creativity, music, and sunshine" according to Graham Nash (member of The Hollies and Crosby, Stills, and Nash). People rarely locked their doors, parties were plentiful, and the musicians jammed together at all hours of the day and night. As it is with most idyllic descriptions of communal life, all was not as it seemed. Although the male musicians in Laurel Canyon could sleep with as many women as they wanted, freed from the bourgeois concept of monogamy, the same rule didn't apply to the women. As the photographer Nurit Wilde put it, "Women were subservient." After Michelle Phillips from The Mamas and the Papas had an affair with her bandmate Denny Doherty, her husband (and bandmate) John Phillips moved into a different house in the canyon. During their breakup, John openly carried on many relationships with various women, while Michelle secretly started seeing Gene Clark of The Byrds. John found out about Gene during a gig, screamed at Michelle, chased her out of the club, and tried to fire her from the band. Recalling life in the canyon, Michelle ironically quips, "There was no free love for me."

It's easy to look at Laurel Canyon and see fallen angels. If only humans were better—less possessive and more expansive in their love—we'd be able to have relationships untarnished by jealousy. Philosophers haven't been so optimistic about this, but not because they think humans are too flawed to manage it. Romantic jealousy is usually a three-party relation between the two lovers and the rival.[14] The lovers are in a reciprocal romantic relationship, and that relationship is exclusive.[15] The lovers love each other especially and they share an intimacy between them that isn't shared with anyone else—they are each other's "special someone." Along comes the rival who threatens to steal the affection of one of the lovers.

There are different ways to be a rival. A rival might want to replace one of the lovers. *She* wants to be the special someone in the relationship and kick the other lover out. A rival might instead just be perceived as a rival by one of the lovers. The rival may be a friend or acquaintance of one lover, and the other lover gets jealous of the affection and intimacy that starts to develop between their lover and the rival. That affection and intimacy might be real or imagined; jealousy can happen in either case.

It's not just romantic relationships that are subject to jealousy. Children are often jealous of their new siblings.[16] One parent can be jealous of the relationship their child has to the other parent. Friends can be jealous of their friend's other friends. Students can be jealous of their classmates who receive special attention from their favorite teachers. The structure is the same as it is in romantic relations: we're jealous of anyone we see as rivals for the attention of someone we want to be special to.

People often assume that the green-eyed monster shows up because something has gone wrong—the relationship is unhealthy or the partner is too insecure. But the possibility of jealousy is there any time you have an exclusive relationship. Jealousy isn't a tarnish on an otherwise pristine love; it's a part of love. There is nothing wrong with wanting to be another person's "special someone." It's not selfish, possessive, or pathological; we just want to be important to the people we love. People who see jealousy as regressive think this desire is immature. Wanting to be someone's one-and-only, so this thinking goes, relies on an idealized conception of monogamous relationships. Jealousy skeptics see no reason to assume that exclusive romantic relationships are the pinnacle of human love. Why can't people love multiple partners at the same time?

The skeptics are correct that romantic depictions of love can be dramatic and overwrought, and there's no need to think that exclusive monogamous relationships are the only model. Does everyone have a soulmate? Probably not—there are lots of people on Earth and you haven't met them all. Even if soulmates are real, there's no rule that says soulmates have to exist in the same time period. Yours might have been a 15th-century sailor who was lost at sea before your great-great-great grandparents were even born (don't ask philosophers to write Valentine's Day cards). Plenty of people live happy and fulfilling lives without getting married or having one life-long romantic partner. Not everyone wants a standard, monogamous long-term love, but everyone wants to be loved and feel special. The need to feel loved and special is what makes us prone to jealousy, even if we can satisfy that need in many different love configurations. Nonromantic jealousy works the same way: we all like knowing that we're someone's favorite.

People who are suspicious of jealousy are quick to call it irrational. They assume that people who are jealous believe that love and affection is a limited resource. The fact that my parents love my sister doesn't mean they somehow love me less, and my friends can have other friends without hurting our friendship. But jealousy isn't this stupid. Our sense of who we are is partly made up of our relations to other people: I define myself in terms of my relationships. I'm my best friend's best friend. If she suddenly starts calling someone else her best friend, who am I now? Until your younger sibling was born, you were your parents' only child. Now the new baby in the house has made you feel like a fifth wheel. You thought you were the funny guy at the office, but the new coworker sure seems to have a knack for making everyone laugh. As our relations change, our sense of ourselves changes along with them. Sometimes those changes are for the better. As Gloria Gaynor attests in the song "I Will Survive," you might be sure you can't live without someone, only to realize that you should have changed the locks when they left. Sometimes we lose someone and we never quite figure out how to rebuild ourselves without them. We just find a way to go on living with a missing piece.

We define ourselves by our relations, but some of them are more central to our sense of self than others. These are the relationships in which we are most prone to jealousy. Building someone else into yourself makes you vulnerable to them. That vulnerability never goes away no matter how secure the relationship is. What it is to love someone is to always be in a position where they can hurt you. Of course, in healthy relationships, they don't want to, but it doesn't mean they can't. When we build ourselves around someone, we want them to build themselves around us, too. We're jealous when we're afraid that our loved ones are attaching too much of themselves to someone else. In order for me to be special to you, our relationship has to be distinct from your other relationships—that's what special means. I want to know that I'm the only one who knows your secrets, the one you come to when you're in trouble, the one who makes you laugh like no one else, the one who knows you better than you know yourself, or the one you can't imagine life without. Sometimes partners *want* their lovers to feel jealousy. If I'm jealous, it means I care about being special to you. It also means that I see how desirable you are: who *wouldn't* want your affection? People tend to think that an absence of jealousy in a relationship is a good thing and that it means the relationship is healthy. But if my partner is never jealous, it might be because he doesn't think anyone else might want me or that losing my affection isn't that big of a deal. He might not be jealous because he doesn't care.

The desire to be the favorite might seem childish, but it's just part of the nature of love. People aren't replaceable.[17] Think of all the reasons you love your special someone. You'll come up with a list of their good qualities—they're smart, insightful, tender, silly, and loyal. Lots of people have these same qualities, and yet you wouldn't trade your special someone for another person with the same list (or even a better list). That's because you don't just love people for their qualities. You love them for who they are.[18] You can fall in love with someone before you even know all their qualities, and you can keep loving them even when they change. You love someone because they're *them*. Because love is particular, we want to believe that our partners can't love anyone like they love us. And maybe they can't, but it doesn't necessarily mean they can't fall in love with someone else and love that person for who they are.

Like all bad feelings, jealousy is painful and hard for us to experience honestly. It's hard to admit that you're afraid of losing your loved one's special attention, and it's wounding to imagine your special someone in the arms of another. If you admit you're jealous, you might start wondering whether you're as lovable as you hope. Given the stigma of jealousy as something dangerous and backward, we hesitate to admit when our eyes start looking a little greener than usual. Coming to terms with jealousy means coming to terms with our flawed conception of love.[19] We imagine love with an unattainable purity—real or true love is never doubtful, questioning, or insecure. It's like a suit of armor, and any instances of worry or doubt are like chinks in its metal. But love is nothing so solid as armor. Loving someone means keeping yourself exposed: always open to the possibility of hurt and betrayal, but trusting that it won't happen.[20] Trust can get shaken and frayed. There is nothing wrong with wanting assurance that our loved ones are faithful and that they still need us as much as we need them. We're afraid of getting our hearts broken, even when we trust the people we love. Feelings of jealousy are just a part of that fear.

Jealousy becomes dangerous and pathological when it isn't paired with genuine concern for the people we love. When someone is afraid of losing their lover's affection, they might try to satisfy that fear at the expense of their loved one's well-being. The possessiveness that sometimes accompanies jealousy is a way of doing something with it: I can shake the fear of losing you if I can just keep you completely to myself. The more I can control who you see and what you do, the less I have to worry that someone else is special to you. Someone who is willing to resort to controlling behavior to alleviate their jealousy has bigger problems than bad feelings. We sometimes try to shake our fears by hurting or besting our rivals. Jealousy between siblings is ripe for this kind of behavior: young children might act out by shoving or hitting their baby brother. It's easier to take your pain out on the person who threatens to steal affection than it is to just sit with that pain, especially when you lack emotional maturity to begin with (that goes for adults as well). Kids, like everyone else, want to feel special, and until the new baby came along, they had every reason to believe they were. People have the expectation that children will automatically love their siblings, but blood relations are no guarantee of love. And it's not just about love. It's about having to learn to play a new role in the family and figuring out how to share life with this new stranger. Children may not have a robust or complex sense of self, but it doesn't mean they have none. Some siblings never grow out of their rivalry, but unless it turns pathological, there's nothing wrong with that. Wanting to be special to your parents means there will always be a part of you that wants to be the favorite. It doesn't mean you hate your sibling or want to hurt them. When your mother gushes over your brother's accomplishments, you might get your feelings hurt and grumble to yourself, "Of course, he's the golden boy." And then you move on with your love for your brother still intact. Sibling jealousy can get distorted just like romantic jealousy, but there is probably more to that story than the feeling. Maybe your parents encouraged competition between you and your siblings, or maybe they were too stingy with their approval. Maybe you and your siblings are just immature, petty score-keepers. Immature people do immature things with their feelings.

Jealousy does its damage when it seeps into other fissures: control, distrust, insecurity, suspicion, manipulation, and dishonesty. We call jealousy the green-eyed monster, but no one ever asks how it grew into a monster in the first place. The philosopher Robert Nozick writes that love "places a floor under" you.[21] Sometimes that floor feels rickety. Jealousy happens because loving someone means living with the possibility that the floor will give way. Vulnerability is the price we pay for love.

Sowing Tares among the Wheat

In the 6th century AD, Pope Gregory I added envy to the list of the seven deadly sins in his *Moralia in Job* (a commentary on the Book of Job). His list of "principal sins" includes envy along with vainglory, anger, melancholy, avarice, gluttony, and lust.[22] According to Gregory, all the principal sins have their origin in pride, which entered the world thanks to Satan's temptation of Adam and Eve.[23] Like an evil tree, the principal sins branch out into more sin. Pride is the root that grows into the list of seven. Then each principal sin gives birth to yet more sinful behavior. Envy causes "hatred, whispering, detraction, exultation at the misfortunes of a neighbor, and affliction at his prosperity."[24] After Gregory's time, vainglory merged with pride and melancholy became sloth in Roman Catholic teaching, but envy has remained on the list ever since.

The English philosopher and scientist Sir Francis Bacon discusses envy in his *Essays, or Counsels Civil and Moral*.[25] Born in 1561, Bacon was a career politician, serving in Parliament under both Queen Elizabeth and James I. His essays are meant to be practical advice, especially for those involved in public life, including monarchs and their ministers. His goal in the essay on envy is to explain how envy works, identify who is most susceptible to it, and tell people how to avoid being its target. Envy happens when we compare ourselves with others: it is "ever joined with the comparison of a man's self."[26] The people most prone to envy are people who do a lot of comparing. For Bacon, that means people who "desire to excel in too many matters" as well as people who are "busy and inquisitive."[27] Envy is a "gadding passion, and walketh the streets, and doth not keep home."[28] If you're minding everyone else's business, you're more likely to get wrapped up in comparison and envy.

Bacon thinks we tend to envy people who are similar to us: "kings are not envied but by kings."[29] Bacon saw a lot of envy in politics where people were often competing for titles and positions. "Men of noble birth" are envious of "new men, when they rise."[30] The faster new men rise through the ranks, the more envied they are (having been a new man himself, Bacon likely knew this from experience). But men who "have joined with their honor great travels, cares, or perils are less subject to envy. For men think that they earn their honors hardly."[31] If you've suffered and overcome many obstacles to get where you are, people are less likely to envy you. Those who don't want to be the target of envy should try not to be showy and should avoid behavior that seems obviously ambitious. Bacon thinks one kind of envy can be beneficial—what he calls "public envy," which "eclipseth men when they grow too great."[32] Public envy is the kind that we feel toward those who are too ambitious. Bacon thinks it can help prevent members of the royal court from trying to climb too quickly through the ranks. The threat that you might become the target of the entire royal court's envy might make you think twice about trying to make a name for yourself. But public envy can become like an "infection" that can "spread upon what is sound and tainteth it."[33] Public envy can end up stifling much-needed new ideas and reforms because it keeps people in line. Widespread public envy also reflects a larger climate of discontent among the citizens of your kingdom, which is dangerous for political stability. Despite his mild praise, Bacon calls envy "the vilest affection and most depraved."[34] He likens it to witchcraft— something not taken lightly in the 16th century—because it has a way of keeping us under a spell. As he describes it, envy "worketh subtly and in the dark."[35]

Bacon's vision of envy isn't that different from our contemporary understanding of it. When you envy your neighbor's new car, you're comparing yourself to them or at least your car to theirs. Since envy involves comparison, we usually compare ourselves to people who are near to us both in proximity (neighbors, coworkers, family) and in status—we usually don't envy kings, as Bacon would say. The more status-conscious you are, the more likely you are to envy. If you're trying to have the best car, the best house, and the best lawn on the block, you'll be paying lots of attention to what your neighbors do. Knowing that your neighbor scrimped and saved for years to buy their new car will probably make you less prone to envy. Our version of public envy is more likely to involve office politics than royal intrigue. You can usually tell when someone is vying for a promotion or is looking to move into leadership positions. If the office climate suddenly becomes chilly toward the openly ambitious person, it might be a check on their behavior. It might also prop up the status quo and keep someone with good ideas from implementing any of them. An office environment where public envy flourishes likely isn't the best place to work.

Most philosophers are happy to keep envy on the list of principal sins.[36] The charges against it are serious: envy prevents you from genuinely feeling happy for other people's successes. It turns your relationships with others into a competition in which someone else's good fortune is a win for them and a loss for you. If other people's successes make you feel bad about yourself, you are probably insecure and lack self-esteem. There are even health risks to too much envy: being "chronically watchful" over your neighbors and your own status increases stress levels.[37] Envy also involves a desire to destroy the object that makes us envious or to harm the person who has it. Unfortunately, envy seems to be as pervasive as it is deadly. Envy or its emotional equivalent is found in a wide variety of cultures and languages.[38] Nevertheless, almost no one thinks envy is good. As the sociologist Helmut Schoeck puts it, "No system of ethics, no religion, no popular wisdom recorded in proverbs, no moral fables, and no rules of behavior among primitive peoples have ever made a virtue of envy."[39]

Although envy hasn't had many defenders, some philosophers agree with Bacon that certain versions of it can be beneficial. Sometimes we can use envy as motivation to improve ourselves. If I envy my neighbor's new car, I might resolve to save up for a new car of my own.[40] Some philosophers have argued that there is a righteous kind of envy.[41] As Bacon argues, we tend not to envy people who have worked hard to get what they have. Much of our envy is directed toward people who don't deserve their success— if they deserved it, we'd be happy for them or we'd admire them. Envy can also be triggered when our circumstances seem unfair. Again, Bacon argues that widespread public envy is a sign that all is not well in the kingdom. Philosophers have argued that a society with lots of envy might also contain lots of unfairness, which means envy might be a warning sign that society is unjust.[42] If society is set up so that some people never have the chance to get what they want, their envy is a protest against their undeserved social inferiority.

You can probably guess by now that I'm skeptical of the "good kind" of envy. In order for envy to be redeemed, so the argument goes, we have to use it to do something good. We either have to use it as "fuel" to improve ourselves or as motivation to address inequality or injustice. If it doesn't meet these criteria, then we banish it to Ovid's dark cave for a feast of snakes. But we can live with envy without defanging it. We all have a vision for how we want our lives to go, and we feel envy when we see someone else enjoying something that is part of our vision. Sometimes our vision for our lives includes very specific things. You might have fallen in love with Cadillacs at a young age—their sophisticated look, their elegant lines, their craftsman-like detail. You pin Cadillac posters to your bedroom walls and resolve that someday you will have one. One day your neighbor rolls into his driveway in a shiny 1957 DeVille—your favorite model. You feel envy because you love Cadillacs and you want one for yourself. Feeling envy when someone else has what you want for your life is a way of caring about that thing and caring about yourself. We long for what we want and don't have, and we can't just smile when we see someone else enjoying it.

Part of envy's bad reputation comes from our criticisms of materialistic desires. Envy, as Bacon points out, is often about status, which means we envy people for status markers like houses, money, and cars. There are fair criticisms to make of materialism: real happiness doesn't lie in having lots of stuff, and people with the most stuff aren't often the happiest. But we don't always envy people for their stuff. We also envy people for their talents, for example, their ability to learn languages, their mastery of the harmonica, or their eye for fashion. Also, there's nothing wrong with caring about stuff. Our sense of ourselves is tied to the objects that we value. The glass you bought on your favorite vacation is how you remember a wonderful time in your life. My prized record collection is how I express my love for music. And the 1957 DeVille is my dream car. We can place too much value on material goods, but valuing material goods isn't always excessive or shallow. If you love and desire something, you won't be indifferent to the sight of someone else enjoying it. You'll be pained because the DeVille is not in your driveway.

Another criticism of envy comes from the fact that it's about comparison. People will admonish you not to compare yourself to other people, but this is wishful thinking. Social comparison is ubiquitous: the psychologist Susan Fiske cites studies where cancer patients compare themselves to other cancer patients to help gauge their illness and their recovery.[43] As the legal scholar Don Herzog writes, "To be a self, to have an identity, is already to have a story about where you stand in all kinds of pecking orders."[44] Comparison isn't always immature jockeying for social position. We all have goals we want to achieve, and we want to feel successful. If you have goals and dreams, at some point you have to ask yourself whether you're achieving them. How do you measure your success? Most of the time we use benchmarks: you're able to run a mile without stopping, you saved enough money for a down payment on a house, or you've gone a whole week without a cigarette. Those benchmarks include comparing yourself to other people. How else are you supposed to know how you're doing if you don't have a standard to compare yourself to?

We tend to think that people who feel no envy are just more mature, less materialistic, and secure in themselves than the rest of us, but maybe they lack envy because they're oblivious, unambitious, or arrogant.[45] Not comparing yourself to others might be a way of avoiding having to face up to your failures or flaws. Comparisons aren't always competitive, petty, or malicious. Sometimes you just need to get a better sense of how you're faring and what other possibilities might be out there for you. We can get too wrapped up in what other people have and don't have, but occasionally looking into your neighbor's driveway can help you figure out what ought to be in yours.

That's well and good, critics will say, but you shouldn't begrudge your neighbor the car. But why? Why can't you be angry, annoyed, or bitter at someone who is relishing something you want? By now, you can predict my saying that there's no reason these bad feelings have to go. The concern most people have with envy is that it will cause you to hurt your neighbor or to do something dastardly to the DeVille. Feeling envy, so this reasoning goes, *necessarily* means wishing that the other person loses the thing you want or wanting to harm the person who has what you want.[46] I think this is mistaking the feeling for how we cope with it. Envy doesn't feel good: we feel it when we feel like a loser because our lives don't look how we want them to look. We're quick to try to do something with that pain.

As you will remember from our discussion in Chapter 3, the most famous envy coping strategy is sour grapes, named for Aesop's fable "The Fox and the Grapes." The fox can't reach the grapes, so he convinces himself they are sour. You tell yourself that the object you lack isn't worth wanting, which helps ease the pain of not having it. As coping strategies go, playing sour grapes isn't the worst strategy. This strategy can be harmless if we add a dose of humor to it. I might look at my neighbor's car and joke, "It's so shiny, it probably hurts his eyes to look at it, poor guy." Normally when we deploy sour grapes, we're lying to ourselves. We're telling ourselves we don't really care about the car even when we do. But sour grapes humor takes the sting away from envy without self-deception. It forces you to laugh at yourself a little.

Wanting your rival to lose what he has and wanting to harm him (or the object) are also coping mechanisms. You might fantasize about a tree falling on your neighbor's new car—wouldn't that just be too bad? Critics of envy are quick to assume this is irrational. A tree falling on the neighbor's car won't suddenly make a new car appear in your driveway. Envious people know this; they aren't deluded. If something happens to the car, I don't have to look at it anymore, and it won't remind me of the things I lack in my own life. The same is true for wanting to damage the object: you walk by the car and think about taking a baseball bat to the windshield. Envy skeptics seem to think that we should never have hostile feelings toward people who are enjoying something we want. We're supposed to smile and be happy for them—how great for my neighbor that he's driving my dream car. This is envy without the venom, which isn't really envy at all.

The fact that you begrudge someone for enjoying something you want doesn't mean you've turned them into a mortal enemy. We can even be envious of people we love.[47] People tend to think there is something especially toxic about envying your loved ones, as though these feelings will forever poison your relationship. But we live with conflicting feelings all the time. You've no doubt been angry—livid, even—at your loved ones and yet loved them at the same time. It might be hard to feel tenderly toward them while you're angry, but love doesn't end where anger begins. Why can't the same be true of envy? Your envy of your loved ones doesn't mean you're not on the whole happy for them. You can have an ache in your heart even while congratulations come out of your mouth. Envy in a relationship, like jealousy, is sometimes a symptom of a deeper problem, especially if you find yourself completely unable to be happy for your loved one at all. But occasional envy doesn't mean love has soured. There's nothing wrong with being pained by seeing someone you love enjoying what you want—just because you care about other people, it doesn't mean you stop caring about yourself. The mistake people make is thinking that feeling envy *has* to mean you want something bad to happen to the person you envy. Hostile feelings are compatible with love, human decency, and respect. When I see my neighbor with the DeVille, I grit my teeth, curse his name, sulk, or shake my fist dramatically (though not when he can see me). And then I go back to my day.

Destructive envy fantasies are mostly harmless. Just like negative emotions themselves, most people have had these thoughts and never acted on them. You indulge a little and then you move on. Destructive fantasies are tempting coping strategies because they give us something to do with our painful feelings. Even the so-called good kind of envy isn't immune from becoming a coping mechanism. My supposedly righteous envy might be self-deception. To deal with the pain of my envy, I tell myself that my rival doesn't deserve what they have—they're unworthy of a Cadillac and can't possibly appreciate it like I do. The same thing is true of the beneficial envy that is supposed to motivate you to improve yourself. You might be pursuing your goal just to best your rival.[48] You'll find a shinier, better DeVille than your neighbor has—that will show them.

The hardest part of living with envy is letting yourself feel it without reaching for a coping mechanism. You don't have to talk yourself out of it, use it as motivation, or convince yourself that the DeVille isn't worth having. We feel envy when we're faced with the realization that our lives don't look how we want them to. Nobody wants to feel like a loser, but that pain is unavoidable. If you care about your life, you can't help wanting to shape it into something you can be proud of. Envy all by itself is no monster. It becomes one when you refuse to live through the painful realization that your life isn't what you thought it would be. You'd rather hurt your neighbor or take a baseball bat to the DeVille than let yourself be fragile. If you're quick to stiffen your upper lip and squirrel more money into the DeVille fund, it might be because you can't stand feeling bad about yourself even for a second. We avoid envy because we avoid feelings of failure. But humans sometimes fail; that's just how life goes.

6

Spite and *Schadenfreude*

The 1949 Academy Award for Best Animated Short Film went to the Warner Bros. Looney Toons cartoon, "For Scent-imental Reasons."[1] It starred Pepé Le Pew, the French Lothario skunk, who was created by animators Chuck Jones and Michael Maltese. Jones and Maltese were thrilled that their producer Eddie Selzer was on stage to accept the award, but not for the reasons you'd think. The Warner Bros. animators had a terrible working relationship with Selzer.[2] He was joyless, arbitrary, and bossy. He interfered needlessly with their creativity, and when he gave them orders, they always disobeyed. When Selzer decreed that there be no cartoons about camels, Friz Freleng wrote a Bugs Bunny short called "Sahara Hare," which featured camels. Selzer then forbade cartoons about bullfighting. Maltese and Jones responded by writing "Bully for Bugs," where Bugs played a bullfighter. Selzer hated Pepé Le Pew, so of course, Jones and Maltese made him the main character in his own Oscar-winning short. Pepé Le Pew, the beloved skunk who brought laughter to millions, is the product of spite.

Unfortunately, other products of spite are not as harmless as cartoon characters. The psychiatrist Jonathan Metzl interviewed groups of White men from Tennessee about health care. All the men suffered from a variety of chronic illnesses, and some of them relied on Veterans Affairs or Medicaid for their care.[3] Despite this, when the topic of government-sponsored universal health care came up, the men decried it as "socialism." They bristled at the thought that their tax dollars would go to support health care for "Mexicans" and "welfare mothers."[4] Ample statistical evidence shows that expanding health care would help the men in the focus group as much as it would help members of racial minorities.[5] The men Metzl interviewed would seemingly rather do without lifesaving care than see someone they didn't like reap the same benefit.[6] Spite can create Pepé Le Pew, but it can also kill you.

Spite and its close emotional cousin, *Schadenfreude* (the German term that we typically translate as "malicious joy"), both take pleasure in someone else's pain. They are some of the more antisocial negative emotions, and that's exactly why the 17th-century philosopher Baruch Spinoza thought they were serious problems.

Spinoza and the "Affects of Hate"

Spinoza was born in 1632 in Amsterdam's Portuguese-Jewish community. He was a bright student and attended Talmud Torah school until his older brother, Isaac, died in 1649. He dropped out of school and helped his father run the family importing business, but Spinoza wasn't suited to be a merchant.[7] In the 1650s, he began studying Latin and became involved in Amsterdam's intellectual scene. Spinoza's new interest in philosophy got him into trouble. He was excommunicated from his synagogue in 1656, and the writ of *herem* (censure) against him proclaims that "all the curses that are written in this book shall lie upon him, and the Lord shall blot out his name from under heaven."[8] What did Spinoza say that led him to be cursed for eternity? His work, *Ethics*, contains some of those controversial ideas. *Ethics* is a somewhat misleading title because the book includes Spinoza's vision of God, the human mind, and the entire structure of the universe. It's also written in the style of a geometrical proof, complete with axioms, propositions, and definitions. It's an unusual book, to put it mildly.

Spinoza is a Controlled Emotions Saint, like Gandhi and the Stoics, which means his views about emotions are linked to his big picture of the universe. Toward the end of *Ethics*, Spinoza describes his version of a model human. The good man is someone who

SPITE AND *SCHADENFREUDE* 125

"hates no one, is angry with no one, envies no one, is indignant with no one, scorns no one and is not at all proud" and who will try to "remove the obstacles to true knowledge, like Hate, Anger, Envy, Mockery, [and] Pride."[9] To achieve this exemplary life, we have to fulfill our highest purpose, which is to perfect our intellect. We do that by contemplating the nature of God. Once we understand "his attributes and his actions, which follow from the necessity of his nature," we will attain a peace of mind that frees us from bad passions.[10] Setting aside whether you believe in God, you might question what exactly Spinoza has in mind here. What, according to him, are the attributes of God, and why does understanding them lead to emotional inner peace?

It turns out God is a substance—in fact, the only substance in the entire universe.[11] 'Substance' in 17th-century philosophy is something of a technical term. Spinoza defined it as "what is in itself and is conceived through itself."[12] In other words, substances don't depend on anything else for their existence. They also contain what philosophers from the time period call "modes" or "attributes."[13] It's not a perfect analogy, but think of it like modeling clay: the clay would be the substance. Clay can take on various sizes, shapes, and colors. Those are its modes or attributes. The clay exists no matter what size, shape, or color it takes, but size, shape, and color can't exist separately from the clay. Modes and attributes are dependent on substances, but substances don't depend on anything.

According to Spinoza, all the objects in the world depend on God for their existence—if it wasn't for Him, they wouldn't be here. Sticking with the (imperfect) modeling clay analogy, God is like a super clay that contains all possible shapes, sizes, and colors simultaneously.[14] All things that exist, from hummingbirds to ham sandwiches, are modes or attributes of God-the-substance. In more traditional theology, God is an all-powerful being who creates the universe and gives it order. For Spinoza, God isn't a separate being; He *is* the universe and its order. His famous phrase to capture this is *Deus, sive Natura* (Latin for "God, or Nature"). Spinoza's conception of God leads him to a view called necessitarianism.[15] For Spinoza, since God is the only substance and everything in the universe is a modification of God, things can't be any other way. The order of the world, just like God, is necessary and eternal, and nothing can change it (you might be starting to see the reasons for the excommunication; Spinoza's views about God are not exactly orthodox).

Since God is the only substance and nothing in the world can be other than it is, humans are simply one part of this eternal structure. That means our emotions (Spinoza calls them "affects"), like everything else, are part of nature.[16] Spinoza thinks of them like natural forces that either help us or hinder us.[17] Good affects, like joy, give us power and energy while bad affects, like sadness, take away our power and energy.[18] We can't make our affects go away, but perfecting our intellect means we will better understand how they work. If we understand that, we'll realize that their true purpose is to help us live well inside the confines of the divine order. Even though you can't change anything about the order of the world, you can still live a good life by gaining a clear understanding of that order. As Spinoza puts it, "True freedom is to be and to remain bound by the lovely chains of the love of God."[19] Remaining bound to our lovely chains means living in harmony with our fellow humans—you can live better in a world where everyone cooperates.[20]

Most of our emotions are obstacles to cooperation, especially the negative ones. All emotions that are what Spinoza classifies as the "affects of Hate" are particularly bad.[21] Included in that list are "mockery" and "disdain," which come closest to our contemporary versions of spite and *Schadenfreude*.[22] Spinoza thinks we always strive to destroy anything we hate and that humans are prone to return feelings of hate with more hate.[23] It's a vicious cycle. The emotions that derive from hate are always bad because they create disharmony among people. If we just understood the nature of God and the universe, we'd realize all this. That's why, according to Spinoza, the good man isn't jealous, doesn't get angry, and doesn't hate anyone. It sounds like a tall order, but if you just read 300 pages of philosophy written like a geometry proof, Spinoza can help you to get the hang of it.

From Spinoza's point of view, spite and *Schadenfreude* are textbook illustrations of human folly. Of all the bad feelings, they might be the most immature. Take the Warner Bros. animators: they had a bad working relationship with their producer. The mature thing to do would be to talk with Selzer like adults and figure out how they could work together. Their disobedience surely made the situation worse. Not only is spite petty, it's also disrespectful. When you're spiteful toward someone, you are deliberately trying to irritate, annoy, or offend them. Jones and Maltese *wanted* Selzer to fume about their disobedience. They delighted in making him angry and were thrilled that he had to accept an Oscar for a cartoon he hated. We often spite people for no other reason besides taking pleasure in their pain and frustration. And the more they suffer, the more we smile.

People who act out of spite will also harm themselves just to get the best of someone else. You can see it in Metzl's health care focus groups. Even though the White men have serious health problems that could be alleviated by better health care, they seem more content to accept their bad fates if it prevents members of racial minorities from benefiting. You've likely heard the idiom "don't cut off your nose to spite your face." You probably also shouldn't deny yourself lifesaving treatment just to make sure someone with a different skin color doesn't get it. Spiteful people hurt others and themselves for nothing. Even if you don't buy into his grand philosophical system, you might think Spinoza had a point: this is lunacy.

Of Human Bondage

One of the most glorious moments in my sporting life occurred in 2018, when I attended my very first Red Sox-Yankees game at Fenway Park. Being in the country's oldest (and obviously greatest) ballpark was thrilling enough, but it was made all the better by the fact that the Red Sox beat the Yankees 15 to 7. Red Sox first baseman Steve Pearce hit three home runs off three different pitchers. My section of the ballpark was even more joyous because there were Yankees fans decked out in their pinstriped replica jerseys sitting nearby. Resounding chants of "Yankees suck" rang out every time the Red Sox scored. The Yankees fans were indignant and miserable, and we relished every second of it.

Sports rivalries are just one of the many places *Schadenfreude* shows up in everyday life. Nothing makes the workday brighter like seeing your least favorite coworker get treated to an epic paper jam courtesy of the office printer. You're pleased to see the driver who cut you off in traffic waiting at the red light ahead. When the cupcakes baked from scratch by the self-righteous super mom go uneaten at the neighborhood block party, you can't help but smirk. You enjoy a hearty laugh when your neighbor who brags about his handyman skills ends up royally screwing up his do-it-yourself plumbing job. Who can resist a little glee when you find out your old high school rival hasn't aged so gracefully?

Why is *Schadenfreude* supposed to be bad? People will tell you that a "bigger person" wouldn't celebrate someone else's failures. The bigger person always sees the pain of their fellow humans as a cause for lament, no matter how irritating those fellow humans are. The ideal we're supposed to strive for is to never make fun of anyone for any reason. "There but for the grace of God go I" or "People who live in glass houses shouldn't throw stones" is what you're supposed to think.[24] If you don't want other people to enjoy your pain, you shouldn't be so gleeful toward theirs.

The bigger person is supposed to have risen above *Schadenfreude's* immaturity, but is that all there is to the feeling? The most common targets of our *Schadenfreude* are people who are a little too sure of themselves. The guy who cuts you off in traffic acts like he's the only person with somewhere to be. The super mom looks down her nose at people who get cupcakes from the grocery store. Your handyman neighbor is a little too loud and proud about his handyman skills. All these people act like they're above us—their attitudes and actions imply that they are better, more important, or more capable than we are. Their self-assuredness feels like it comes at our expense. We feel pleasure at their minor failures because their inflated egos get deflated back down to normal size.

Philosophers are divided on this feature of *Schadenfreude*. Some have argued that it's a sign of low self-esteem.[25] The attitudes and actions of others shouldn't affect our sense of self-worth. If I'm bothered by my neighbor's haughtiness over his handyman skills, it must be because I'm insecure about my own. *Schadenfreude* is a reflection of your own low self-worth, and that's something you should fix. Other philosophers think *Schadenfreude* can be righteous because we feel it toward people who deserve their suffering.[26] Their pain is like poetic justice, and we're simply approving of them learning their lesson. An example of righteous *Schadenfreude* is the kind we feel at the downfall of the hypocrite, like Jimmy Swaggart, the 1980s televangelist.[27] Swaggart publicly accused Jim Bakker, a fellow televangelist, of sexual immorality (in what was likely an effort to oust him and take over his ministry). Shortly thereafter, photos emerged of Swaggart in a hotel room with a prostitute. A slick, power-hungry TV preacher who points the finger at other sinners turns out to be one? If you don't feel *Schadenfreude* at that, you had better check your pulse.

But not all *Schadenfreude* is about low self-esteem or poetic justice, for example, sports. Anyone who thinks Red Sox fans suffer from low self-esteem hasn't met any Red Sox fans. They think the baseball world revolves around Boston. Sports *Schadenfreude* also doesn't have much to do with justice. As much as Red Sox fans are fond of referring to them as "The Evil Empire," the Yankees aren't bad humans. Even the most die-hard Red Sox fan will admit that Mariano Rivera was one of the best closers and a classy guy to boot. The Yankees don't "deserve" to lose, even though I'm thrilled when they do.

It's true that the common targets of our *Schadenfreude* are people who think they're better than we are, but it's a mistake to think that this reflects low self-esteem. Caring about yourself means that you'll take offense when someone looks down their nose at you, even when they don't come right out and say it. Critics of *Schadenfreude* seem to expect that we ought to have no reaction at all when someone else is haughty and that reacting to it means we don't have strong enough barriers around ourselves. But why is it a good thing to erect barriers? Other people affect you because you care about being a part of social life with them. You see yourself as a human among fellow humans. If you're invested in relationships with others—even when those relationships are casual—their attitudes will mean something to you. Of course, we can get too wrapped up in everyday human drama, but being enmeshed in social life means you're vulnerable to what other people think and do, even if you feel great about yourself. Being a self in the world is not like viewing human social relations from inside a glass box. Selves are porous and other people seep in, but a porous self isn't a weak self. It's just the price we pay for being part of human social life.

Most cases of *Schadenfreude* are not grand enough to qualify as justice. It's notoriously about small things like traffic, block parties, and plumbing jobs gone awry. We even laugh at the pain of people we love: imagine your friend walks into a party, trying to look cool and sophisticated, only to run face first into sliding glass door. There's no sense of desert here and you don't want them to be hurt, but you can't help laughing at their failed attempt to put on airs. Telling ourselves that our pleasure in another's pain is actually justice might just be a way of rationalizing our cruelty.[28] If I convince myself that my least favorite coworker deserves to be bested by the office printer, then I can tell myself I'm justified in cheering their frustration. Making *Schadenfreude* about poetic justice ultimately turns it into Lowly Worm—all cleaned up and working in service of the good. It takes away what is impish in *Schadenfreude*. That impishness is precisely what people criticize, but that's because they think the glee we feel is more malicious than it is. People who warn against *Schadenfreude* assume that, since we're all flawed humans, we shouldn't laugh at other people's flaws. It's the equivalent of living in a glass house and throwing stones. But you could have many attitudes toward your common flawed humanity. One of them is bemusement and Montaigne was a master at it.[29]

One of Montaigne's most famous essays is "On the Cannibals." Montaigne knew about the discovery and conquest of the New World (the Americas) in the 15th and 16th centuries. He read a book by Girolamo Benzoni, a merchant who had traveled to the Americas and had seen some of the horrors visited upon the indigenous people by the Spanish colonists.[30] Montaigne thought it was ironic that some Europeans were appalled at the reports of cannibalism among indigenous people and yet somehow not appalled by the massacres perpetrated by the conquistadores. Montaigne would have none of this prejudice: he writes that "every man calls barbarous anything he is not accustomed to."[31] He points out that indigenous people lack some of the vices that European society has—no one over there lives in poverty or goes hungry.[32] Of course, they have violence and bloodshed, but this fact doesn't trouble Montaigne. What does trouble him is that "while judging correctly of their wrongdoings, we should be so blind to our own."[33] Montaigne asks what is more barbaric: to eat someone after you've killed him or torture him on the rack and burn him alive, like Europeans do?[34] Montaigne spends the rest of the essay arguing that much of what the indigenous people do is equal to or better than what Europeans do. He ends the essay with a joke: "But they wear no breeches."[35] They can't possibly be like us because they don't wear pants.

Montaigne's essay is a humorous call to Europeans to get off their high horses. Montaigne thinks every human society has its idiosyncrasies and its corruptions—societies are imperfect because people are imperfect. No one gets to claim that their customs are the pinnacle of human achievement and that everything else is savagery. If you do, you're taking yourself too seriously. Montaigne's antidote for this self-seriousness is humor. We all need to learn to laugh at ourselves because no one is above human imperfection. We're all together in the thick of human folly, and if you think you've somehow gotten away clean, you'd better take another look at yourself.

Schadenfreude is one way our laughter at ourselves manifests. Critics assume we're laughing at others because we're forgetting that we're capable of the same blunders. I think we're laughing *because we know* we're capable of the same blunders. The targets of our Schadenfreude are the ones who act like they're above it all, but we know differently—they're down here in the muck with the rest of us. When they fall on their faces, our Schadenfreude is an emotional "I told you so." The idea that we should only feel compassion for our fellows when they pay for their own foibles makes human imperfection into a kind of unfortunate accident—we fall victim to it like we fall victim to an illness. But that's not how human folly works. No one is immune from it, but sometimes we're messes of our own making. We usually make our biggest messes the moment we think we're incapable of making them. We don't have to treat human imperfection with kid gloves to acknowledge that none of us are above it. Critics of Schadenfreude tend to think that it's like living in glass house and throwing stones, but I can laugh at a fool while at the same time knowing I've been a fool myself. Schadenfreude is a way of recognizing that everybody plays the fool.

I'll Show You

Montaigne thinks that one of the quirks of human nature is that our desires are strengthened by frustration. Is a pleasure easy to obtain and plentiful? Then we no longer want it.[36] The food in your fridge is never as appealing as the food in a restaurant, and the books on your shelf don't seem as interesting as the ones in the bookstore. People enjoy romantic trysts arranged in secret all the more because they feel forbidden—it "gives smack to the sauce."[37] Montaigne will be the first to admit that he becomes a contrarian around people who are too sure of what they believe: "You make me hate things probable when you thrust them on me as infallible."[38] Telling him some claim is indubitable is the surest way to make him doubt it. Montaigne speculates that his château might have survived attacks during France's civil wars precisely because he chose not to barricade it: "Defenses attract offensives."[39] There is no thrill in conquering an opponent who openly lays down his weapons.

Humans have a defiant streak and spite is part of it. If *Schadenfreude* is an emotion that lies in human connectedness, spite is an emotion that recognizes we also need our space. Most of the time we spite people who boss us around or butt into our business. The Warner Bros. cartoonists became spiteful toward Eddie Selzer when he told them what not to draw. Chuck Jones had no plans to write a cartoon about bullfighting until Selzer told him not to. He may not have even *wanted* to write about bullfighting, but Selzer's prohibition made bullfighting suddenly irresistible. It didn't matter what Selzer ordered. Jones would have drawn whatever Selzer told him not to draw *because* Selzer told him not to draw it. And Jones wanted Selzer to know that he was defying his commands on purpose.

One of the major criticisms of spite is its imprudence: we do things that are bad for us just to spite someone else. I'll do whatever you tell me not to do, even if what you tell me to do is good for me. You might advise me to skip dessert because you genuinely care about my health. I might also care about my health, but if you're too bossy about the dessert, I'll order it anyway, lower cholesterol be damned. Spinoza would argue that doing what you know isn't in your best interest is the peak of irrationality. Because I care about myself, so his reasoning goes, I should always want to do what's good for me. But self-love is more than just concern for my health and welfare. Caring about myself means I want to be the one in charge of how my life goes. It's not enough for me to be happy and healthy. My life has to be *mine*; it has to belong to me.

If Montaigne's *Essays* has a theme, it's learning how to live with yourself. That's not an easy task. We are constantly drawn in a thousand directions away from ourselves. Since Montaigne was involved in politics, he saw first-hand how ambition pulls people into social climbing and constant jockeying for rank.[40] You might think everything will be fine if you just stay out of politics, but Montaigne says: think again. Our "domestic tasks" may be less important, but they are no less demanding on our time and attention.[41] We get caught up in daily household drama—mowing the lawn, soccer practice, neighborhood gossip—and lose ourselves as easily as do the ambitious people in politics. You can't hide from life's demands, and things don't magically become better just because "we have changed our landscape."[42] The real problem is inside you, and you can't run from yourself. So, what do we do?

Montaigne thinks we have to figure out how to take ourselves "back into possession" and draw ourselves back from all the places we've been pulled.[43] His famous metaphor for this is the room at the back of the shop: "We should set aside a room, just for ourselves, at the back of the shop, keeping it entirely free and establishing there our true liberty."[44] You need a place in your head or in your soul where you can be you alone with yourself. You have to make sure you can still hear your own voice when everyone is shouting at you, and your room is a place where other people's voices don't reach. Having this room isn't about withdrawing from life into perfect solitude. The room at the back of the shop goes with you wherever you go—PTA meetings, diplomatic missions, and the night shift. It's not about being a hermit. It's about not losing sight of who you are.

We feel spite when someone tries to barge into our room at the back of the shop. Of course, it's smart to eat healthy and I may even want to do it for myself, but if too many people start wagging their fingers at me, I'll make the opposite choice just so I know the choice was really mine. It might matter more to me that I decide something for myself than that I do the smart thing. Spite is a way of asserting that my life is mine to live and that I'm the one who gets to decide who I am. Sometimes we're contrarians just to be contrarians, but that behavior isn't always pointless disagreeing. Being a contrarian might be helping me make sure my mind is still my own—it's my way of asserting my will, just to feel that it's there. It's because I care about myself and my life that I don't always take it well when other people demand things of me. Spite is a way of saying, "You're not the boss of me." Refusing to be ordered around or told what to think can be a way of keeping the room at the back of the shop intact. We are usually spiteful toward people when it feels like they are trying to barge in—overbearing bosses, finger-wagging parents, and holier-than-thou neighbors. If it feels like someone is encroaching too far into the boundaries I'm trying to set, spite is the emotion that says, "back off."

Like all emotions, spite and *Schadenfreude* can become destructive and distorted, but they usually aren't the source of the problem. We're more apt to see ugly versions of spite and *Schadenfreude* when social life becomes adversarial.

Bite the Hand that Feeds

Montaigne lived during France's civil wars, which were between the Protestant Huguenots and the Catholics. The violence was sporadic but severe.[45] One of the most famous events was the St. Bartholomew's massacre in 1572, where Huguenot nobles had been invited to attend the Catholic royal wedding of King Charles IX's sister. After the wedding, the king had the nobles executed. News of the murders spread throughout France and set off waves of violence. Catholics feared a Huguenot reprisal, so they went on the offensive. Anti-Protestant mobs made up of private citizens went from house to house in Paris, dragging Protestants into the street,

killing them, and dumping their bodies into the Seine. The violence spread into other French cities, like Bordeaux and Toulouse.
Montaigne was horrified by all of it:

> I live in a season when the unbelievable examples of this vice of
> cruelty flourish. . . . If I had not seen it I could hardly have made
> myself believe that you could find souls so monstrous that they
> would commit murder for the sheer fun of it; would hack at an-
> other man's limbs and lop them off and would cudgel their brains
> to invent unusual tortures and new forms of murder, not from
> hatred or for gain, but for the one sole purpose of enjoying the
> pleasant spectacle of the pitiful gestures and twitchings of a man
> dying in agony, while hearing his screams and groans.[46]

Aside from the gore, one of the difficult parts of the war was never
quite knowing which side people were on. Montaigne wrote, "The
worst part of these wars is that the cards are so mixed up, with
your enemy being indistinguishable from you by any clear indi-
cation of language or deportment."[47] Protestants and Catholics
didn't wear uniforms, and they both spoke French. When you traveled around the country, as Montaigne frequently did, you had to
watch what you said because you never knew whether the person
you were talking to would suddenly draw a sword on you. What
made matters worse, according to Montaigne, is that opposing
sides would switch positions depending on what their enemies
did: "First, remember which side, only last year, was mouthing
the affirmative, making it the buttress of their faction, and what
side was mouthing the negative, making their buttress out of that.
Then listen from what quarter comes voices defending which side
now, and whether they are rattling their swords less for this side
than they did for the other!"[48] What was blasphemy last year is or-
thodoxy today. When my enemies employ a dirty tactic, they are
heretics, but when my side does it, we are following God's com-
mand. Montaigne thinks most of the professed religious zeal of the

warring factions is specious. In reality, it's just that "Christians excel at hating enemies."[49] God's will is important, but not as important as the chance to run my enemy through with a sword.

Polarization in contemporary life probably looks tame from Montaigne's point of view, but its focus is also hating the enemy. Political scientists in the United States have debated the role of partisanship—a strong identification with a political party—in political life for many years.[50] Political differences seem to have become more partisan over time. Instead of making decisions about who and what to vote for based on policy, more people are making those decisions based on their identity as party members. As political scientist Lillana Mason puts it, "our conflicts are largely over who we think we are rather than over differences of opinion."[51] Partisanship isn't confined to politics. Americans managed to turn soda into a partisan feud during the Cola Wars between Pepsi and Coca-Cola in the 1980s.[52] If we can do that, we can make teams out of pretty much anything.

A common explanation for partisan vitriol involves what psychologists call "intergroup dynamics."[53] Red Sox fans are my "ingroup," and the Yankees fans are the "outgroup."[54] Some psychological studies purport to show that intergroup dynamics are deeply ingrained in us. They're supposed to arise out of more basic features of our psychology, such as our need to belong and our tendency to organize the world into categories.[55] Researchers did brain scans of Red Sox fans and Yankees fans and had them report their emotional responses after viewing various plays. Both sets of fans felt similar pleasure at seeing their team win and at seeing the rival team lose.[56] In a different study, subjects who watched a film of people getting their hands pricked by a needle often exhibited a sympathetic hand twitch—unless the hand on the screen had a different skin color from theirs.[57]

It's tempting to look at these studies and think that intergroup hostility goes very deep into human nature and history. My "Yankees suck" chants harken back to the time of prehistorical tribal warfare and my need to disparage them is "hardwired" into my brain. We tend to appeal to prehistorical or evolutionary explanations whenever human behavior seems confounding. Since we can't really say why the people in the red hats hate the people in the blue hats, it must be "tribalism."[58] The talk of evolution or deep features of human psychology gives us the illusion that our intergroup hostility is instinctual and therefore irrational. But tribalism is at the same time usually lodged as a criticism; it's behavior we're supposed to guard against. If we can avoid it, it must not be so hardwired after all.

When we call something tribal, we're almost never referring to something we're doing. Tribalism is always someone else's problem—*those* people are tribal, but, by a magical somehow, *we* are not. Even if it's true that human beings have a need to belong and tend to organize the world into categories, tribalism as an ideology doesn't automatically follow from these facts. Humans evolved to have depth perception, and we've used it to paint and do archery, but that doesn't mean painting and archery are necessary consequences of our depth perception. Appeals to tribalism give us a special term to describe intergroup hostility, but they don't help us do anything about it.

The increasing vitriol on display in public life is sometimes explained as a problem with negative emotions. Mason argues that the more sorted into groups we become, "the more emotionally we react to normal political events."[59] Even if they don't cause partisanship, these feelings are thought to be a major driver in it. We seem to revel in our outrage at what the other side is doing and in our glee when they fail. The frantic pace of cable news and social media allows us to keep constant tabs on our enemies' next nefarious move. But the story is more complicated than "bad feelings make us do bad things."

Spite and *Schadenfreude* happen when selves get together with other selves in social life. Self-building isn't a purely private affair. Figuring out who I am means figuring out my place in the world among other humans. I want to feel understood and feel like I belong. If other people understand me, it can help me understand myself. Of course, when we interact with other selves, we don't always like what we see. When I encounter someone whose self is very different from mine, it affects me in both good and bad ways. That's especially true if that self seems to be built in a way that conflicts with my sense of self. If I see someone wearing a shirt that says "philosophers are egg-sucking dogs," I can't be indifferent to it. It might make me laugh, it might make me angry, or it might confuse me (who even makes shirts like that?), but it will make me feel something—about myself and about the person wearing the shirt.

Because selves are porous in this way, it's easy to feel like other people are encroaching on your sense of self. This happens in part because of how we display ourselves in public. Self-expression is part of self-building; we want to show other people who we are. We figure out ways to display things about our identity as we move about the world, so we use symbols of self-expression, like bumper stickers.[60] Bumper stickers announce things about you to anyone who sees the back of your car—you love camping or you've run a marathon. But there is a downside to symbolic display. Bumper stickers are a form of shorthand: they distill some aspect of your identity down to a picture or slogan. That means they leave a lot of room for interpretation on the part of the viewer. You see my "I heart camping" sticker and imagine me as a crunchy, hippie tree-hugger who probably hates big trucks (like the one you happen to be driving). Bumper stickers don't invite you to think about the complex human driving the car. They invite you to slot that person into a type or a kind.

Symbolic self-expression extends far beyond bumper stickers. People draw conclusions about who we are based on what kind of car we drive, what street we live on, what clothes we wear, what TV shows we watch, and where our kids go to school. Sometimes people draw the conclusions you want them to draw: I want you to see my Red Sox hat and conclude that I'm a baseball fan and they're my favorite team. Sometimes they draw conclusions that you might not intend. My "I heart camping" sticker comes across as some sort of challenge to your sense of self. You read me as one of those outdoorsy types who probably looks down on your comic book collection or as a self-righteous environmentalist who loves lecturing people about using too much plastic. When we read symbolic displays as challenging to ourselves, we sometimes make counter-displays: "Oh, that's who you are? Well, let me tell you who *I* am." Of course, someone else's self-expression doesn't have to threaten mine. The fact that I love camping doesn't mean I hate your comic book collection or that I want to thrust a metal straw into your mouth. But our bumper-sticker mode of self-expression lends itself to unnecessary hostility, especially if social relations are already tense.

Spite and *Schadenfreude* show up when self-building gets adversarial, but they aren't the cause of the hostility. When Metzl listens to the White men in his focus group, he finds people who feel like they've been caught in a world of winners and losers.[61] They feel like their way of life is eroding and they don't belong. To use the sociologist Arlie Hochshild's metaphor, they feel like they've been patiently waiting in line for their turn at the American Dream, but the line doesn't seem to move and other people seem to be cutting in front of them.[62] Feelings of disorientation and unfairness are painful and hard to live with. It's easier to find someone to blame than it is to face the fact that you don't understand your place in the world anymore. If I'm being made uncomfortable, then there must be someone who is being made comfortable at my expense. Politicians looking for votes, cable news shows grabbing for viewers, and social media platforms hungry for clicks are all happy to confirm your suspicions. You start looking at the world through a film of paranoia. *Those people* are moving to your town and taking opportunities that were supposed to be yours. Everyone seems to be encroaching on your way of life, and you don't want to be left with the booby prize.

Of course, a good long look at American history shows us that women and members of racial minorities—the people who often end up taking the blame for the discomfort—have been the ones whose comfort in the world is sacrificed for the comfort of others. They aren't cutting in line; they're finally being allowed get in the line after being kept out the whole time. Everyone wants to belong and have space to build their own lives. The fact that more people are making room for themselves in social life doesn't mean they're treading on you. You don't get to demand that other people build themselves to your specifications just so you don't have to feel uncomfortable. The person wearing the "philosophers are egg-sucking dogs" shirt doesn't get to prevent me from being a philosopher just so they can have the world to their liking. The fact that other people build their selves differently from yours doesn't mean you lose and they win. Self-building isn't a sport, but when people have been made to feel like social life is a competition, it can become one. Once I start looking at the world through the paranoid film, my own self-expression becomes a way of besting the people I see as trespassers in my world.

For Montaigne, this is what happened with the Christians in the religious wars who excelled at "hating enemies." Both sides focused far more on casting the other side as destroyers of the Good and the True than they did on trying to be good Christians themselves. They convinced themselves that, *in order to be* good Christians, they had to vanquish their enemies. The more heathens they killed or maimed, the better Christians they were. This is how we end up with distorted forms of spite and *Schadenfreude*. When your understanding of who you are depends on frustrating the people you define yourself against, your own commitments and values become an ever-moving target. In the French civil wars, one side's beliefs became entirely dependent on just being the opposite of the what the other side believed. But that just means you have no real commitments at all. If your opponent says the sky is blue, you'll deny it just to avoid agreeing with them. Your beliefs become mere contradictions with no substance. An identity built on spite and *Schadenfreude* is just as hollow. Living just to see someone else cry isn't much of a life.

There's nothing wrong with feeling spite and *Schadenfreude*, but they aren't made to bear the weight of a self. Partisanship is bad because it means we've collapsed our identity into something empty. If you build your whole self around being someone else's hater, you'll need to make sure that your enemies are losing or failing so that you can keep your sense of self intact. You'll always be on the lookout for the next pain or frustration you can revel in. Once you've built yourself around a conflict, you have every reason to keep the conflict going. What happens if you win and defeat your opponent for good? There's nothing left of you. That's no way to live. Selves need to be made out of stronger stuff than being your enemy's enemy. We all need to be more than our bumper stickers.

7

Contempt

In 1913, a devil baby was born in Chicago.[1] Rumor had it that he was taken to Hull House, a live-in charitable organization run by the philosopher and peace activist, Jane Addams. Addams and her staff had heard nothing of the devil baby, but some of the women from the Italian immigrant community that Hull House served were sure he was there. They described "his cloven hoofs, his pointed ears and diminutive tail; moreover, the Devil Baby had been able to speak as soon as he was born and was most shockingly profane."[2] Word spread about his alleged existence. Repeated denials that there was in fact a devil baby couldn't deter visitors from flocking to Hull House for six straight weeks. It turns out "people of every degree of prosperity and education" wanted a look at the demonic infant.[3] Addams's staff fielded constant inquiries from people asking to see the devil baby or demanding to know where he was hidden. She listened to them "repeating for the hundredth time that day, 'No, there is no such baby'; 'No, we never had it here'; 'No, he couldn't have seen it for fifty cents.'"[4] Addams recognizes that people are naturally curious, but she confesses that "as the empty show went on day after day, I quite revolted against such a vapid manifestation of an admirable human trait."[5] The devil baby wasn't real, but people rarely let a little thing like evidence get in the way of their conspiracies.

Addams's reaction to the people looking for the devil baby can fairly be described as contempt. We can imagine her sighing with exhaustion at yet another knock at the door. The staff probably had more than one laugh at the expense of the saucer-eyed visitors trying to catch sight of a tail or a cloven hoof. On their more frustrating days, you can imagine them exasperatedly imploring people to just use their brains for once. Contempt is in all of these expressions; it has a wide variety of looks. We can see it on the face of the sneering butler, the haughty mean girl in the school cafeteria, the smug intellectual, and the half-mocking pity of parents to their melodramatic toddlers. It comes out as an eyeroll, a scoff, and an upturned nose. Plenty of people think contempt shouldn't come out at all, no matter what it looks like. Among the negative emotions, contempt is especially potent. Philosophers have described it as a "deep dismissal, a denial of the prospect of reconciliation, a signal that the conversation is over."[6] Not everyone is so suspicious of contempt. Aren't there times when we *should* end the conversation? Do we just have to constantly put up with bigots, conmen, and believers in devil babies? Can't we just wash our hands of them and walk away?

Like most of our quandaries about bad feelings, the contempt question has been around for a long time. One of its heydays was in the 18th century.

Rousseau and Wollstonecraft: Blighting the Tender Blossoms

Jean-Jacques Rousseau was born in Geneva in 1712.[7] Hardship visited him early: his mother died ten days after he was born, which left him in the care of his father and his aunt. His father fled Geneva when Rousseau was only 10, and Rousseau took various apprenticeships to help support himself. At the age of 16, he was taken in and financially supported by a wealthy noblewoman, Francoise-Louise de la Tour, Baronne de Warens. The Baroness saw to it that he finished his education but also eventually became his lover. Rousseau moved to Paris and made a modest living as a tutor. He was involved in the Parisian intellectual scene with fellow French philosophers, Denis Diderot, Etienne Bonnot de Condillac, and Voltaire (with whom he developed an ugly and life-long feud). Rousseau's radical writings, along with his ornery and polemical personality, got him into trouble. His novel, *Emile,* and his treatise in political philosophy, *The Social Contract,* were condemned and publicly burned in Paris. He tried to flee home to Geneva only to find that his works were condemned and burned there as well. Rousseau took refuge in Scotland and lived (briefly and unhappily) with fellow philosopher David Hume. He eventually snuck back into France, went into hiding, and assumed a fake name. He died suddenly in July of 1778.

Many of Rousseau's philosophical contemporaries argued that high culture, art, and society were positive influences on human beings—they make us refined, cosmopolitan, and civilized. Rousseau argued the opposite: high culture and society corrupts our otherwise naturally good disposition. In particular, social life creates in us a distinctive and dangerous passion: *amour-propre,* which is a bad kind of self-love or vanity.[8] *Amour-propre* is what leads us to think about ourselves in comparison and rivalry with others. In social life, we find human beings "subject, by virtue of a multitude of fresh needs, to all of nature and particularly to his fellowmen."[9] Rousseau's contrast to this civilized man is a figure he called "savage man," an idealized version of a person who existed prior to the formation of society. Savage man knows "neither vanity, nor deference, nor esteem, nor contempt."[10] He doesn't compare himself to other people or see himself in terms of social rank. Once societies are established, however, we start caring about our status: "As soon as men had begun to mutually value one another, and the idea of esteem was formed in their minds, each one claimed to have a right to it."[11] Once social status starts to matter to us, we become entangled in an arms race of wealth, power, and rank. For Rousseau, this is degenerate. We'd be happier and kinder to each other if we didn't vie for honor or esteem. The emotions that surround our need to compare are likewise degenerate. Feelings of contempt are both unnatural and vicious.

Mary Wollstonecraft, Rousseau's English contemporary, didn't quite share his pessimistic views about contempt. Wollstonecraft was born in London in 1759 to a struggling middle-class family.[12] She left home at 19 to eke out a living as a governess and a teacher before getting a paid position at a radical periodical called *Analytic Review*. She married fellow journalist and writer William Godwin, even though they had both argued against marriage in print. Their marriage was happy and egalitarian, and they both maintained social and economic independence. Sadly, the happiness ended quickly: Wollstonecraft died in childbirth just five months after they were married (the daughter she bore became Mary Shelley, the famous author of *Frankenstein*). Wollstonecraft defied the gendered expectations of her day in nearly every way. She earned a living working in the male-dominated world of publishing, she was outspoken in politics, and she cherished her independence more than anything. She was a well-known critic of inequality and a fierce champion of women's rights. The English writer Horace Walpole once referred to her as "a hyena in petticoats."[13] I like to think she took it as a compliment.

Wollstonecraft agrees with Rousseau's criticism of our need for wealth and status: "From the respect paid to property flow, as from a poisoned fountain, most of the evils and vices which render this world such a dreary scene to the contemplative mind."[14] We want to be admired for the things that signal our standing in the social hierarchy, and we end up having contempt for others who don't have high standing. In our rush to acquire wealth and property, we turn our energies away from what really matters. Never one to mince words, Wollstonecraft claims that all the positive attention we pay to the wealthy is a "true north-east blast that blights the tender blossoms of affection and virtue."[15] She argues that the "preposterous distinctions of rank" will "render civilization a curse by dividing the world into voluptuous tyrants and cunning, envious dependents."[16] Philosophers in the 18th century were particularly concerned about upper-class attitudes to the poor. Wealthy people's contempt for the poor prevented them from seeing poverty for the social ill that it was.

Wollstonecraft feared that contempt would turn the poor into a permanent social underclass. In the 18th century, there were few avenues for upward social mobility—if you started at the bottom of the social ladder, chances were high that you'd stay there. Since everyone wants esteem, you'd naturally seek out the esteem of your peers, but what secured you esteem in a low social class wouldn't secure you esteem in a high one. To use a contemporary example, my upper-class colleagues expect me to be able to talk about opera and would be unimpressed by my extensive knowledge of heavy metal. If somehow you could make it into a higher class, nothing in your experience would prepare you for that new world. You'd seem like an alien from another planet to your new peers. They would then use your social ineptness as proof that poor people were fundamentally different in some way—poor people just aren't capable of cutting it in high society, no matter how much wealth they acquire.

Wollstonecraft thought women were trapped in this exact dynamic. Because women were told that their only proper domain was keeping a fine house, they had thrown themselves into these meaningless pursuits, which rendered them incapable of doing anything else. When they tried to learn about other things, like politics or philosophy, nothing in their background had prepared them for these new worlds. So, they ended up floundering, much to the amusement of their male counterparts. The result is that "they must, from being treated like contemptible beings, become contemptible."[17] Wollstonecraft sees the cycle of contempt as a detriment to the overall health of society.

Given her criticisms, you might assume Wollstonecraft would try to convince us to get rid of contempt altogether, but you'd be mistaken.[18] She thought contempt could be justified and nothing illustrates it better than her essay "A Vindication of the Rights of Men" (an earlier companion piece to her famous work "A Vindication of the Rights of Women"). The essay is a response to the philosopher Edmund Burke's 1790 essay, "Reflections on the Revolution in France," which is about the French Revolution in 1789. Burke's essay attacked a good friend of Wollstonecraft's (Richard Price) and expressed skepticism about the enterprise Wollstonecraft was devoted to: individual rights and liberty. She makes plain from the beginning of her essay that she plans to show contempt for Burke's writing. She warns, "if, therefore, in the course of this epistle, I chance to express contempt . . . I beseech you to believe that it is not a flight of fancy."[19] In other words, if you read contempt in Wollstonecraft's voice, you better believe she means it. She calls the arguments in Burke's essay "pretty flights" that arise from his "pampered sensibility," and claims that he allowed his emotions to "dispel the sober suggestions of reason."[20] She marvels at the fact that the "ripening judgment of sixty years" (Burke was 60 years old) had not managed to tame Burke's "teeming fancy."[21] She says she won't take the time to refute all of Burke's arguments because "it would be something like cowardice to fight with a man who had never exercised the weapons with which his opponent chose to combat."[22] Translation: if they were in a duel, Wollstonecraft would have a broadsword and Burke would have a wet noodle—it just wouldn't be fair.

If Wollstonecraft is worried about the dangers of contempt, why does she try to eviscerate Burke with it? What Wollstonecraft laments about contempt is not that we feel it, but that we feel it toward the wrong things. We *should* have contempt for vice and folly.[23] Wollstonecraft thinks Burke deserves her contempt because Burke's own essay was full of contempt and ridicule. A pompous jerk doesn't deserve a gentle response. Wollstonecraft agrees with Rousseau that status-seeking corrupts our emotions, but instead of getting rid of contempt, she thinks we just need to correct it.

Both Rousseau and Wollstonecraft agree on some of the basic features of contempt. Like envy, it's an emotion that involves comparison, and the contemptible person comes up short.[24] We see the contemptible person as beneath us or beneath whatever standard we're comparing them to. The expressions of contempt communicate the low status of the contemptible person: we look down our noses, tell them they aren't worth our time, or we simply turn our backs on them and walk away. Rousseau and Wollstonecraft disagree over what we might call contempt's proper object: what are we supposed to have contempt for? Even though our feelings sometimes get corrupted by our status-seeking, Wollstonecraft thinks contempt's proper object is vice or folly, like the kind Burke displays in his writing. By her lights, Burke failed to meet standards of civility and integrity. If he's willing to stoop to such lows, then we should see him as contemptible.

Like Wollstonecraft, some contemporary philosophers have defended a righteous version of contempt.[25] Righteous contempt is directed toward people who fail to meet basic standards of character or who have no principles. Spineless toadies, merciless opportunists, and smarmy confidence men are all examples of fair targets for contempt because they have no integrity. People who deserve contempt are those who stoop low. Contempt seems especially justified if someone else directs it at you first. The philosopher Macalester Bell has defended what she calls "counter-contempt," especially as a response to racism.[26] You'll remember Anna Julia Cooper's experiences with train conductors who showed racist contempt for her by folding their arms and refusing to help her get off the train. Defenders of righteous contempt would say that Cooper has every right to show the conductors contempt in return. The conductors wrongly treat her as lesser, so she is under no obligation to be respectful or polite to them. They don't deserve civility.

Rousseau objects to all of this (at least in theory; in practice he had no trouble displaying contempt). He thinks contempt isn't the sort of emotion that can be righteous. Contempt's proper object isn't vice; it's inferiority. All there is to contempt is feeling superior to someone else. Rousseau would happily point out that we feel contempt for people for all sorts of reasons that have nothing to do with vice. Shabby clothes? Terrible at dancing? Kind of funny looking?

All these are targets for contempt. Contempt is about hierarchies, and social life can make hierarchies out of lots of things. We might feel contempt toward people who lack character or integrity, but we also feel it toward people who are ugly, poor, and stupid—things they can't easily change about themselves. As philosophers in the 18th century knew, even though the wealthy had contempt for poor people, poor people didn't "deserve" contempt. Wollstonecraft would say that this is contempt gone awry and that only contempt toward vice is justified. But Rousseau thinks contempt can never be justified—it's about vanity, not virtue. For Wollstonecraft, contempt is like a firehose: it's fine if you point it at the right thing, but you can do damage if you point it at the wrong thing. For Rosseau, contempt is like a tidal wave. There's no right way to use it; all it does is destroy.

Of Blue Skies

I have an on-again-off-again relationship with yoga. I have tried and failed to stick with it multiple times in my life. I am neither graceful nor flexible, and nothing about me can be honestly described as serene. Of course, this is precisely why yoga would be good for me. While I was writing this book, I decided to join a local studio to see if I could finally commit to it once and for all. The studio was close to a large university, so many of my fellow attendees were college students or graduate students, who were easily 20 years my junior. Our yoga instructors would remind us not to worry about what other people in the class were doing: "Just focus on your own practice and take what you need." It's a helpful mantra that is easily forgotten when your neighbor is twisted into a pretzel and balancing on one arm while you can't even manage to touch your toes.

Occasionally there were other people in the class who shared my struggles. I was always grateful for their presence because they made me feel better about my own feeble abilities. When someone else in the room looked like the Tin Man from *The Wizard of Oz*, I wasn't alone. It was even better if they were worse at holding the poses than me. If they sweated and wobbled more than I did, I was able to comfort myself with the thought, "Well, I'm not *that* bad." I knew I wasn't as good as most people in the class, but I knew I was better than somebody. My attitude toward my fellow inflexible classmates was contempt—a mild version and maybe not very malicious, but contempt all the same.

Most people have had experiences with contempt like mine and are probably shy about admitting it. Contempt is one of the negative emotions that falls prey to the extreme cases problem I mentioned in Chapter 2: we tend to define negative emotions by their most serious and damaging instances, like Iago's envy. When we think of contempt, we usually imagine the most severe types, such as the contempt that people feel toward other races or ethnic groups. Focusing on these examples makes it seem like contempt is an attitude you only take toward someone else if you see them as less than human. Just like the other negative emotions, we have far more experience with the milder versions, but we rarely think of them first.

Contempt is about looking down on people and it's everywhere.[27] It's no accident I felt contempt in my yoga class—exercise culture is full of it. When I started running (the only form of exercise I've ever managed to stick to), I would visit online running communities for tips. There was lots of support for new runners and people who were struggling to improve. It often took the form of the mantra: you're lapping everyone on the couch. Even if you're not as good at running as you want to be, you're still doing better than the "couch potato." In my morning yoga class, my instructors would sometimes say things like, "You're here practicing before some people have even gotten out of bed." It was a way to remind us that, even if we were struggling, we were making more of an effort than someone else. Contempt is in parenting: you don't make baby food from scratch every day, but you pat yourself on the back when you see other parents feeding their kids junk food. Contempt lives in your neighborhood. I may not have a fully restored 1957 Cadillac DeVille in my driveway, but at least I don't have an ugly clunker sedan like that loser down the street has. Contempt shows up at work. Your least favorite coworker starts presenting another one of his "brilliant" ideas in a meeting and you think, "What an idiot." You may not be perfect at your job, but you wouldn't do that.

At the heart of contempt is a feeling of a self-assuredness that we get from looking down on others—*I'm not like that.*[28] I call it the "blue sky" of contempt, drawn from a passage from W. E. B. Du Bois's *The Souls of Black Folk.* In one of the essays, Du Bois tells a story about the first time he notices racist contempt from his White classmates. The children were exchanging visiting cards (like business cards, except for individuals rather than businesses), and his was rejected out of hand by a White girl. After that moment, Du Bois began to realize that because of his race, he was "shut out from their world by a vast veil."[29] The veil is Du Bois's metaphor for the separation he feels between himself and the world of White people. He describes the feeling of the veil as "measuring one's soul by the tape of a world that looks on in amused contempt and pity."[30] Du Bois responds to his realization this way:

> I had thereafter no desire to tear down that veil, to creep through; I held all beyond it in common contempt, and lived above it in a region of blue sky and great wandering shadows. That sky was bluest when I could beat my mates at examination-time, or beat them at a foot-race, or even beat their stringy heads.[31]

Du Bois responds to the White world's contempt for him with contempt of his own. He reassures himself of his own worth by besting his White classmates in all competitions. Throughout his youth, Du Bois used this strategy whenever he felt the weight of the veil. He imagined himself as "drawn up into higher spaces and made a part of a mightier mission."[32] Occasionally, he even felt pity for his White classmates "who were not of the Lord's anointed and who saw in their dreams no splendid quests of golden fleeces."[33] He convinced himself that he wasn't part of the White world because he belonged somewhere higher, somewhere better. If White people failed to appreciate him, it was because they simply couldn't see his greatness: "Whatever racial feeling gradually crept into my life, its effect on me in these earlier days was rather one of exaltation and high disdain. They were the losers who did not ardently court me and not I."[34]

Du Bois's blue sky illustrates the core feature of contempt. When we feel it, we feel self-satisfaction in comparing ourselves to others because we come out looking better. The fact that contempt involves this kind of superiority and comparison makes people nervous. As we saw in Chapter 5, envy has the same problem. Despite how frequently we compare ourselves to others, everyone tells you that you're not supposed to do it. And you're certainly not supposed to use someone else's struggles to make yourself feel better about your own.

But where does self-confidence come from? How do we acquire it? We know what the end result is supposed to be: you're supposed to keep your eyes on your own yoga mat and focus on your practice. But how do you manage to get there? If selves are the sorts of things we have to make, self-confidence is likewise constructed. This is precisely what Du Bois does. From behind the veil, Du Bois can't help but wonder about his self-worth. Who is he that a classmate would refuse his visiting card without a second glance? Faced with these incidents, Du Bois does what most of us would do: he responds to self-doubt by trying to find evidence that he's succeeding somewhere. If he manages to beat his classmates at academics and in physical contests, then he must be good at *some* things. He has to compare himself to others to figure out whether he has any strengths. Once he's successful in the competitions, he sees his achievements as evidence that the White world simply doesn't appreciate him the way they should. His contempt is an expression of his newfound self-assuredness.

That's fine, you might think, but Du Bois was a child when he found his blue sky, and only children build self-confidence through comparison. Adolescence is a shark-infested sea of constant ranking based on the thinnest and shallowest metrics. How, your teenaged-self might have asked, can I show my face in ninth grade with a backpack like *this*? Those of us who have sailed to stiller waters are no doubt breathing sighs of relief that we no longer engage in these kinds of comparisons. When your sense of self is shaky and barely formed, you might be monitoring everything your peers are doing and trying to figure out what it says about you. Once you become more settled in your sense of self, you stop paying so much attention to what your neighbors are doing. You start focusing more on what's right for you and your life and on measuring your success in different ways. You're supposed to eventually make your way out of the comparison game. Isn't this what we should all be striving for?

The problem is that there is no magical time in your life when you finally, once-and-for-all feel sure of yourself. Of course, we do grow out of the adolescent phase (at least some of us do), and it becomes easier to keep your eyes on your own yoga mat. But that doesn't mean your sense of self will never feel shaky again. Any new phase in your life introduces new doubts. You start a new career or get promoted, and suddenly you find yourself feeling like a rookie again. You move to a new city and can't even manage to find your way to the grocery store without getting lost, much less figure out how to meet new people. You have a baby and you mine books for answers to questions you didn't even know existed. Your parent falls ill and you feel like you're lost in a maze of medications, paperwork, and hospital hallways. Self-confidence isn't like reaching a summit where you can stand back and enjoy the view. It's like owning a house: it requires maintenance. Sometimes everything works fine and you don't have much to do. Other times you finish installing a new roof only to discover a leak in the water heater. Every time you reach a new stage in your life, take up a new activity, or go through an unexpected event, you'll find yourself wondering whether you're doing things right. You'll make comparisons to gauge your progress, and feelings of contempt will come right along with them.

Sometimes you're advised to only compare yourself with your past self—as long as you're doing better than you were yesterday, that's all that matters. It sounds high-minded, but it could also be narcissistic: thinking that you're only in competition with your former self might just be a way to dodge criticism. Interacting with other selves in the world opens up possibilities that aren't visible from where we're standing. If I only focus on what I'm doing, I might not see that better things are out there for me. Comparing your life to someone else's can help you realize that you need to make some much-needed changes. People usually tell you not to compare yourself to others when they're trying to make you feel better about your struggles. Don't worry about those 20-somethings next to you in yoga class who can put their feet behind their heads. "Don't compare yourself to them" is sound advice if you're using comparisons to beat yourself up or if you're not giving yourself enough credit for your own hard work. But other people aren't background noise; you can't just tune them out. Building a self is hard. We're works in progress and we don't know if we're making a masterpiece or a mess. Comparing ourselves with others helps us measure our progress and gives us some clue about how we're doing.

It's not just comparison that makes people wary of contempt. It's that we end up feeling superior to others—we are looking down, after all. Looking down on people seems to violate a sense of equality and community that we're supposed to have with our fellow humans. If you don't want someone looking down on you, you better not do it to someone else. It's a mistake to think that comparisons are always petty or malicious; often we find camaraderie in them. Even though I'm happy to see someone else struggling with yoga, I feel more in common with them than I do with my pretzel neighbor. The more mundane versions of contempt are compatible with treating our fellow humans as equals. Human social life is rife with comparison, but that's because we're all trying to build selves together. If you feel like you have no idea what you're doing, comparing yourself to others can give you a sense of direction, but we have to remember that we aren't always on the good end of the comparison. One day we might find ourselves in the shoes of the people we look down on. *I'm not like that* doesn't mean *I'll never be like that*. We ought to keep our comparisons in perspective, but that doesn't require us to get over contempt. We just have to feel it with a healthy dose of self-awareness.

Of course, sometimes our feelings of contempt make us judgmental and holier-than-thou. Contempt can certainly be malicious, but often the bigger problems are the judgments that trigger it. Is the problem with a racist that they feel contempt or that they think members of different racial groups are beneath them? Racist beliefs are bad no matter what emotions accompany them—whether it's contempt, anger, or pride. Contempt causes trouble when we use it to convince ourselves that we'd never be contemptible. Every time we look down on someone else, another person is probably looking down at us. My pretzel neighbors probably used my struggles to boost their self-confidence on their rough days, and I shouldn't forget that when I'm using the struggles of someone else to feel better about my own.

Contempt helps us gain self-assuredness when we need it. It buys us some much-needed confidence when we can't find any inside ourselves. Like all negative emotions, contempt can't bear the weight of an identity. Building your sense of self around looking down at other people will trap you in the shark-infested waters of adolescence, constantly looking over your shoulder to see what everyone else is doing. Contempt gives us a compass—a way to get our bearings. But there won't be some shining moment when we'll never need contempt. There will be no time in our lives when our sense of self is permanently unshakable. New phases of life will unmoor us, and we'll find ourselves directionless again.

The Revenge of the Devil Baby

What about the more severe versions of contempt—the dismissive kind we feel when we decide that certain people are beneath us and we refuse to waste our time on them? We might get to the point when we throw up our hands and say, "That's it, I'm done with you." If people insist on believing in the devil baby even though it's ridiculous, past a certain point we may just reach the end of our emotional rope.

Addams's essay about the devil baby is actually a trick. Upper class, educated Chicagoans looked down their noses at the immigrant community in the city. While Addams tried to help this community, the surrounding communities didn't think they were worth helping. She was used to hearing talk about how "we" don't want "those people" around. Addams knows her readers would react to the story of the devil baby with contempt, so, at first, she pretends to feel the same way. As the essay proceeds, she slowly tries to get the reader to take the perspective of the immigrants who are curious about the devil baby. She observes how the older women in the community were deeply affected by the incident. They start to open up about their own lives and Addams listens to their stories. She realizes that many of them "had been forced to face tragic human experiences; the powers of brutality and horror had had full scope in their lives, and for years they had had acquaintance with disaster and death."[35] These women had come to a country where they had no work and didn't speak the language. They had been in abusive marriages and had children for whom they struggled to provide. They had cared for sick relatives without access to medicine. They knew what it was like to have almost no power to "subdue the fiercenesses of the world about them."[36] As she retells the stories of the women, she realizes that there is more to their interest in the devil baby than superstition. She starts to understand what the devil baby really represents, and she is able to see what might bring someone to believe in it. The devil baby was symbolic; it reminded the women about how little control they had over their own lives. Her feelings of contempt ebb once she starts to see the world through the eyes of the devil baby believers.

The defenders of righteous contempt will ask: why should we extend this kind of sympathetic understanding to people, especially when they don't deserve it? What about the bigots and conmen of the world? In public life, we are confronted by hateful, ignorant views espoused by hateful, ignorant people. If they refuse to treat others with respect, why not simply turn up our noses and walk away? Aren't we justified in showing contempt for some people?

Addams and Du Bois were part of a philosophical movement known as American pragmatism (along with William James, whom we met in Chapter 2). Like all philosophical groups, the pragmatists don't all agree, but one of the common themes among their ideas is the importance of democracy. Democracy, for the pragmatists, isn't just a form of government with representation and elections. Democracy is a way of life: it's a commitment we make to ourselves and each other to live together in a way that recognizes the humanity of everyone. For the pragmatists, democracy requires that we to try to understand the wide array of experiences of our fellow humans. Addams thought democracy required an "identification with the common lot" of everyone in social life.[37] We can only identify with each other if we genuinely try to understand each other's lives. Addams warns that if "we grow contemptuous of our fellows," we will "tremendously circumscribe our range of life" in a way that threatens our commitment to democracy.[38] For Addams, looking down your nose at someone prevents you from seeing through their eyes.

Du Bois is likewise skeptical of the idea of righteous contempt.[39] After he tells the story of his blue sky, he writes, "Alas, with the years all this fine contempt began to fade; for the worlds I longed for, and their dazzling opportunities, were theirs [his White classmates], not mine."[40] He contrasts himself with "other black boys" who "shrunk . . . into silent hatred of the pale world about them and a mocking distrust of everything white."[41] In his later works, Du Bois explains that he tried to keep up the same attitude of contempt once he reached graduate school at Harvard. Rather than participating in the social life on campus, he withdrew, describing himself as "conceited enough still to imagine, as in high school, that they who did not know me were the losers, not I."[42] But he admitted that his withdrawl from campus social life was driven by a fear of rejection: "I was desperately afraid of not being wanted . . . of appearing to desire the company of those who had no desire for me."[43]

Seventeen years after *The Souls of Black Folk* was published, Du Bois wrote a book called *Darkwater*. It contains an essay called "The Souls of White Folk," which is a companion piece to the essay in *Souls* where Du Bois's blue sky of contempt appears.[44] "The Souls of White Folk" opens with the image of Du Bois in a high tower above "the loud complaining human sea."[45] He explains that he has a special vantage point where he can see into White people's souls: "I see these souls undressed and from the back and side. I see the workings of their entrails. I know their thoughts and they know that I know."[46] In spite of this, White people attempt to hide themselves from Du Bois's view: "they preach and strut and shout and threaten, crouching as they clutch at rags of facts and fancies to hide their nakedness."[47] Even though Du Bois can see through them, they hold on to the assumption that "of all God's hues whiteness alone is inherently and obviously better."[48] Du Bois watches them from his tower with "tired eyes."[49] In the opening of the essay, White people are depicted as laughable and ridiculous. In the same way they look at him with "amused pity and contempt" in *Souls*, he now sees them as objects of contempt.

Whiteness doesn't remain ridiculous because "after the more comic manifestations . . . come subtler, darker deeds."[50] White people expect anyone who isn't White to gratefully accept their subordinate status. When Black people decide to question the presumed superiority of Whiteness—when they insist "on [their] human right to swagger and swear and waste"—the White people respond with insults, hatred, and violence.[51] Du Bois is angry at the suffering he experiences as the target of the hatred, but he also feels "a vast pity—pity for people imprisoned and enthralled, hampered and made miserable for such a cause, such a phantasy."[52] Du Bois closes the essay with the image of himself in the tower again. He watches "the great ugly whirlwinds of hatred, blood and cruelty," and yet he also refuses to believe that they are inescapable: "I will not believe that this is all that must be, that all the shameful drama of the past must be done again today before the sunlight sweeps the silver seas."[53]

Du Bois no doubt felt contempt for the White world. At the beginning of his life, his blue sky served him well. It allowed him to maintain self-confidence at a time when he desperately needed it. But eventually he realized that his self-confidence alone wouldn't bring him the real opportunities to participate fully in the world the way he wanted to. His contempt wasn't going to change the fact that the White world tried to shut him out. The White world was inescapable in both a practical sense and an existential sense. In a practical sense, Du Bois was clear that White people had "annexed the earth and hold it by a transient but real power."[54] There was nowhere he could go to escape White supremacy forever. In an existential sense, his fate and the fate of White people were intertwined. Du Bois writes, "I am related to them and they have much that belongs to me. . . . I share their sins."[55] Having contempt for the White world meant trying to keep it at a distance and trying to set it apart. But Du Bois's life was entangled with the White people, and whether they wanted to admit it or not, their lives were entangled with his. He couldn't just walk away, and neither could they.

There is no doubt that sometimes we reach the end of our rope with people. You might have had to cut a family member out of your life after years of painful conflict. You might not be on speaking terms with one of your coworkers after months of disrespect. In its mild forms, contempt is a way to build self-confidence. In its more severe forms, contempt can be a way of protecting ourselves from harm or denigration. Trying to maintain a relationship with someone who constantly attacks your self-worth takes too much of a toll. Sometimes cutting people off is the only way we prevent further damage to ourselves. Contempt's blue sky can look a lot more like a bomb shelter. We often find ourselves feeling contempt when the rest of our emotional well has run dry. After the shouting and tears, there is nothing left except the stone-faced resolve to not let this person have any more of my life than they've already taken.

But it's a mistake to think that contempt like this is justified or righteous. Sometimes it's our only option if we want to protect ourselves, but we shouldn't pat ourselves on the back for feeling it. Divorcing yourself from a fellow human isn't cause for congratulation, even if it turns out to be necessary for your self-protection. If there is anything that Du Bois sees clearly, it's that the cycle of contempt is a tragedy. He thinks we need to try to find a way out of it—to not repeat "the shameful drama of the past." Du Bois is clear that part of the problem with racism is that it is built on the lies White people tell themselves about Black people. White supremacy is a delusional "phantasy," and the contempt White people show to Black people is part of the attempt to prop up the lie. Unfortunately, this dynamic is more widespread than it ought to be:

> All this goes to prove that men are . . . woefully ignorant of each other. It always startles us to find folks thinking like ourselves. We do not really associate with each other, we associate with our ideas of each other, and few people have either the ability or the courage to question their own ideas.[56]

Even if contempt can help us build self-confidence and help us protect ourselves, that doesn't mean we ought to be happy cutting people off, especially in public life. For Du Bois and for Addams, a commitment to democracy means that we try to get beyond the images we create of other people. Addams knew that many early 20th-century Americans thought immigrants were beneath them.

Du Bois knew that White America harbored racist contempt toward Black America. Both Addams and Du Bois think of themselves as speaking for groups of people who the rest of society finds contemptible, and they try to send the same message: don't dismiss, try to understand.

When we talk about contempt in public life today, who are the contemptible people in society now? Taking a cue from Wollstonecraft, defenders of righteous contempt might answer that only people who are vicious are *rightly* contemptible. Unlike the groups that Addams and Du Bois wrote about, vicious people don't deserve sympathy or understanding. The problem is that who counts as vicious will change depending on who you ask. There is a contingent of Americans, which is larger than I would like to admit, that believes egghead professors like me are destroying the fabric of society. Defenders of righteous contempt will say these people are wrong, and I'd like to agree, but figuring out who the real villains are isn't a task that is left up to a select few. Public life doesn't work that way: we all get to pass judgment on each other.

It's not as though there's never a right answer about who the bad guys are, but as a group, human beings have made mistakes in the past and have labeled some people villains who didn't deserve it—just ask Addams and Du Bois. We don't always get it right, and the self-assuredness of contempt—*I'm not like that*—can be dangerous when it's about our own righteousness. We're often at our worst when we're sure we have the high ground. If that's our reality, we had better make sure the judgments we pass are at the very least informed and that we make some effort to defend them against scrutiny. That means we'd better understand the people we're judging, even if they're egghead professors.

For the pragmatists, a commitment to democracy requires understanding, but understanding doesn't translate into acquiescence. Addams tries to understand why the devil baby holds such a fascination for the older women in the community, but that doesn't mean she suddenly believes in the devil baby herself or that she's not annoyed at people who demand to see it. It's fair to expect people to support their beliefs with evidence and to not hang on to beliefs they know to be false. It's fair to expect that people won't look down their noses at someone else because of their skin color. Realizing that our lots are cast together doesn't mean we never judge each other. But, as Du Bois sees clearly, it also means we can never really rid ourselves of each other, no matter how much we'd prefer to.

We only feel secure in looking down on people when we're sure we're on the top rung of the ladder—that we'd never be in the same category as the bigots or the conmen. We pride ourselves on not associating with "those people." The problem is that, in somebody's eyes, all of us are potentially one of "those people." When we defend righteous contempt, we usually assume that we're the ones looking down our noses. Suppose instead that you're the one on the receiving end of righteous contempt: how would you want people to treat you? Would you want people to pat themselves on the back for washing their hands of you? Would you want people to judge you without trying to understand you first?

If there is no such thing as righteous contempt, people tend to draw the conclusion that we shouldn't feel it at all. But this isn't right. What was true for our other bad feelings is true of contempt: our emotions don't have to be righteous in order for us to value them. Contempt is a part of our lives because we compare ourselves to others. Comparison is part of self-building, and contempt helps us build self-confidence. If I can see that I'm doing better than someone else, it helps me convince myself that I'm not a total screw-up. That can be especially helpful when I'm full of self-doubt. And self-doubt is a persistent feature of being a human in the world. Every new phase of life introduces new uncertainties, and we're not always sure that we're headed in the right direction. Being able to say *I'm not like that* lets us get our bearings. Like all the other bad feelings, contempt can get twisted—we can use it to convince ourselves that we're always on the top rung of the ladder. But contempt isn't to blame here. Sometimes people who are full of contempt are just caught up in the same sad status game that plagues adolescents—just replace having the coolest backpack with having a house in the best neighborhood or a degree from the "right" university. Even if it's not about status, contemptuous people are usually trying to build their whole selves around *I'm not like that*. But defining yourself according to who you're not never tells you who you are. Just like the other bad feelings, you can't build a self out of contempt. It can be a part of our lives without becoming the lynchpin of our identities.

Sometimes contempt is the only way to protect ourselves from further damage. When abuse, disrespect, and manipulation wear us down to a nub, contempt gives us shelter to salvage what's left. But this doesn't make contempt justified or righteous; it just means we need it to keep ourselves intact. We can accept that contempt plays this important role without congratulating ourselves for it. You can save yourself by burning a bridge, but you're still only left with ashes.

Conclusion

Loving the Wild

We've taken a closer look at some of the worms in the garden and have tried to get to know them a little better. Now that you've come face-to-face with them, you have a decision to make. What will you do with them? If I've convinced you that you shouldn't get rid of them and you shouldn't try to tame them, you might think all you can do is to accept them. Fighting them is useless and might even cause more harm than good. Maybe if we stop trying to wrestle them into submission, they won't do too much damage in our lives.

But this isn't right. Your negative emotions aren't an unfortunate fact that you just have to face. Remember that Nietzsche's edict *amor fati* translates to "love of fate." You should love the worms in your garden, not merely tolerate them. We need to stop hoping that if we quit fighting our bad feelings, they'll lie quietly and behave. Loving the worms means loving them as they are—dirt, slime, and all. We need to, as Nietzsche puts it, "work honestly together on the task of transforming the passions of mankind one and all into joys."[1] How do we do this? If we're going to change our relationship to our bad feelings, we need to uncover some of the assumptions we're making about ourselves and about what our lives are supposed be like.

Drenched in Reality

Henry David Thoreau, the 19th-century American philosopher, walked into the woods near Walden Pond on July 4, 1845.[2] He dug his own basement, built his own house using old lumber, and cut down trees to make his own furniture. He hunted and fished, and planted a garden of beans, corns, peas, turnips, and potatoes. Although he kept up his social life in the nearby town of Concord, Massachusetts, Thoreau spent most of the next two years in the woods. He called his time on Walden Pond his "experiment."[3] It started out as an experiment to "transact some private business with the fewest obstacles" but became much more.[4] Thoreau came to realize that he went into the woods to learn how to live. He wanted to live deliberately, not to watch his life "frittered away by detail."[5] Thoreau had serious doubts about the value of the civilized village life he experienced in Concord. He had graduated from Harvard and had aspirations to become a writer. He had little success, despite having famous friends like Ralph Waldo Emerson. He upset the townspeople with his odd demeanor and abrasive behavior—he refused to vote, attend town meetings, or pay his taxes.[6] By the time he went to live in the woods, he had earned the reputation among the people of Concord as a lazy, talentless, ornery ne'er-do-well.[7] But Thoreau wasn't interested in being accepted into Concord social life. Thoreau's era was marked by growth and economic prosperity, which gave birth to new ways of marking social status.[8] Everyone, it seemed to Thoreau, was clamoring to make more money so that they could buy more things. He worried that "men have become tools of their tools."[9] Was there nothing more to being alive than working harder and harder so that you could have more fashionable clothes or a bigger house? Thoreau wanted more than this. As he describes it, "I wanted to live deep and suck out all the marrow of life."[10] So, off he went to live in the woods, to work and live just for himself.

Thoreau's experiment gave him a new appreciation for the wild—the natural world around him, but also the wild in himself. When people want to escape the humdrum of their lives, Thoreau writes that they like to imagine "rare and delectable places in some remote and more celestial corner of the system."[11] But Thoreau discovered that Walden Pond was "pasture enough" for his imagination.[12] His cabin was part of the woods that surrounded it. Birds became his neighbors, and the pond itself had a life all its own. He noticed how the water changed with the seasons, how in the fall the water became so still that it was "a perfect forest mirror."[13] At daybreak, the pond would throw off "its nightly clothing of mist . . . its soft ripples or its smooth reflecting surface was revealed."[14] Living in the woods showed Thoreau that the fantastical and the spiritual aren't out there in the expanses of the universe. They are right here, all around us. People are more apt to seek meaning "in the outskirts of the system, behind the farthest star," but Thoreau thinks real meaning lies in the "perpetual instilling and drenching of the reality that surrounds us."[15] In one of the famous passages in *Walden*, Thoreau says that living in the woods helped him find two different parts of himself:

> Once or twice . . . while I lived at the pond, I found myself ranging the woods, like a half-starved hound, with a strange abandonment, seeking some kind of venison which I might devour, and no morsel could have been too savage for me. The wildest scenes had become unaccountably familiar. I found within myself, and still find, an instinct toward a higher, or, as it is named, spiritual life, as do most men, and another toward a primitive rank and savage one, and I reverence them both. I love the wild not less than the good.[16]

Thoreau doesn't merely accept or tolerate his wild part. He loves it. He loves it because he comes to see the wilderness—both inside and outside himself—in a new light. Living in the woods gave him a chance to really get to know the wilderness, to learn its rhythms, and to see that it wasn't as dangerous as some people feared. He also realizes that the wilderness inside of him isn't something to be feared: it's just as central to who he is as his higher, spiritual side.

What if Thoreau is right, not just about himself, but all of us? We all have a wild part inside of ourselves and it's where our bad feelings live. What would it take for us to love it like he does? First, we'd have to give up the aspiration to emotional sainthood—not because it's not possible but because it isn't worth wanting. It only seems attractive because we think the alternative is to be bogged down in the worst parts human life. Emotional saints think giving up your bad feelings frees you from the petty, mean, and small-minded concerns of human life. As a result, you get to enjoy a kind of blissful peace where nothing ever ruffles your feathers. Achieving the blissful peace is supposed to give your life a new or different kind of meaning. But you're not trading one kind of meaningful life for another; you're giving up a meaningful life that is fully human for one that isn't. The blissful peace that the emotional saints promise comes at the cost of the meaning *this* life has. But you have to care about your life as it is in the here and now to live it well or to live it *at all*. That means you have to be fully immersed in the human world and vulnerable to every part of it—the tragic, the joyous, the strange, and the mundane. And if your life matters to you, bad feelings will be a part of it. Emotional saints might try to convince you that you can have it both ways and love this life while also getting over your bad feelings. But choosing to live fully in human reality is a package deal. You can't tell people to find joy in all the little things, but then tell them they can't find anger in the little things. Negative emotions are ways of caring about your life. You either care about it, and so welcome the worms in your garden, or you try to drive out the worms by caring less.

Maybe I've convinced you to reject emotional sainthood, but what then? We still have work to do to love the wild in ourselves. One of the biggest challenges we face to living well with our bad feelings is being afraid of what they'll do to us and to other people. I've argued that you don't *need* to tame your bad feelings, and Thoreau doesn't try to tame his wild part either. He writes, "We are conscious of an animal in us. . . . It is reptile and sensual, and perhaps cannot be wholly expelled. . . . I fear it may enjoy a certain health of its own; that we may be well, yet not pure."[17] Well, yet not pure is the perfect way to describe living well with negative emotions. Giving up emotional sainthood means giving up the idea that purity is better. Being well is enough. Bad feelings are not stopping you from having a good life. Their presence isn't a sign that something is wrong with you. When your negative emotions show up, they are doing exactly what they are supposed to do: signal your attachment to yourself and your life. So, let them do that, even if feeling them scares you. At times, you too might feel like a half-starved hound looking for venison to devour, but why should you never feel that way? We think bad feelings are bad because we think they mean something they don't—that if we feel spite or jealousy, it's because we're bad people. But if emotions have a life of their own, this can't always be true. Sometimes you'll feel spite and jealousy in spite of yourself. And there's nothing wrong with that because bad feelings aren't the monsters that we think they are. They can be hard to handle, but that just makes them wild, not bad.

We have no reason to expect that being fully human in the world will always feel calm and peaceful. That's wishing for purity. Being well and not pure means realizing that immersion in the real human world will come with a huge range of complex, difficult emotional experiences. Your emotions won't always be positive; they might shock you, and overwhelm you. But why is any of this a problem? If you're invested in life, your emotions will respond to all the things that happen in it. And life is complicated. It's not always positive, it's shocking, and it's overwhelming. Is it surprising that our emotional life will reflect that? Really caring about something opens you up to strong feelings. Have you ever loved someone or something so much it scared you? You might have been afraid of how vulnerable or consumed you felt, but also exhilarated and alive. If even love can feel dangerous, why can't negative emotions feel the same? The emotion double standard will tell you that love does no harm, but bad feelings do. Like most wild things, negative emotions cause problems because we won't leave them alone. All by itself, anger doesn't do anything other than tell me that I feel slighted or harmed. It doesn't have to be anything more than that. Instead of letting my anger just be what it is, I jump to conclusions about it or try to turn it into something else. I worry that it's a sign of my flawed character, I'm afraid that I'll fly into a rage, or I think I'll feel angry forever if I don't nip it immediately. I make it into a justification for lashing out, proof that someone else is my enemy, or evidence of my own superiority. Even when negative emotions are big and powerful, there's no reason to panic. Resist the urge to do something with them. Learn how to just feel.

Just feel—it's harder than it sounds. Letting our emotions be what they are requires us to accept that they have a life of their own. Their independence challenges our conviction that we are always in control of who we are. It's an easy assumption to make: we make a lot of decisions. We're under pressure, both internal and external, to construct a plan for our lives. It starts early: people ask children, "What do you want to be when you grow up?" As you get older, that plan is supposed to become concrete and you're supposed to take the steps to make it happen. Some of my college students are sure that they have failed at life if they don't know what they want to major in by the time they finish moving into their dorm rooms. Succeed in school, find a partner, establish a career—this is life's normal trajectory. Once you finish school, people will ask you about a job. Once you find a job, people will start asking you about your relationship. Once you find a partner, people start asking about kids. Even our mundane daily lives are made up of hundreds of tiny decisions— what to eat for dinner and what brand of trash bags to buy. This constant stream of choosing can sometimes lead us to think that we're completely in charge of who we are and how we live. But that's not quite right. Sometimes we're forced to make certain choices: the company I work for wants me to relocate and I don't want to quit my job, so off I go. We simply find ourselves attracted to particular people or activities. It's not as though I decided one day to fall in love with my husband; it just happened. As our relationship developed, he became the center of my world, and now I don't know what life looks like without him. But it wouldn't be right to say that I chose to build him into my life the way I did. Of course, I chose to marry him and chose to stay with him, but I can't really say I chose to love him. The same thing happened when I became a philosopher: I chose to get a PhD and apply for jobs at colleges, but I didn't decide to love philosophy. I was captivated by it—it got its hooks into me when I took my very first class. Finding meaning in things is a complicated mix of choices and feelings.[18] Families, lovers, friends, children, pastimes, and passions—we decide to commit to them, but also our hearts are captured by them.

Facing the independence of your emotions means admitting that something at the core of who you are and what matters to you isn't fully up to you. That might seem too precarious: feelings can be fleeting and fickle. Will I just wake up one day and my love for philosophy will be gone? Here's the scary answer: maybe. It happens more than you think. People wake up after years of marriage and realize they're no longer in love. One day you discover that you don't have the passion for your career that you once did. Parents-to-be genuinely worry that they won't love their children. These thoughts are terrifying, which is why we're so reluctant to face them. We don't want to admit that the meaning in our lives partly depends on something we can't control. We spend a lot of time (and sometimes money) trying to stave off this thought. It's how the ethos of "lifehacking" gets traction. As the communications scholar Joseph Reagle describes it, lifehacking treats everything as a system, something "modular, composed of parts, which can be decomposed and recomposed . . . governed by algorithmic rules, which can be understood, optimized and subverted."[19] The self-help industry is saturated with lifehacking techniques: boost your productivity in three easy steps; use this one weird trick to make your chores a breeze; this app will show you how to find love. The premise behind all of this is that there is some code to making your life work out exactly how you want. All you have to do is crack it. Cracking this code means nothing is out of your control, but an emotional life with its own rules threatens that. So, we then try to crack the code inside ourselves. If I download a mindfulness app, follow bite-sized bits of New Stoicism, or beat myself every time I have a bad feeling, then I'll always be in control. This isn't just a fantasy. It's tragic. Never wanting to be out of control keeps the richness of life from really touching you. You avoid the garden altogether for fear of the dirt.

Human emotional life is a complicated thing. We don't always know what we feel, and we don't always feel what we think we should. Sometimes we feel consumed by our emotions. Sometimes we beg for them when they don't come. But, as Thoreau put it, they make us well, yet not pure. You'll feel pain, heartbreak, rage, jealousy, and all the rest because that's what happens when you care about human life in all its fragility and unpredictability. Loving the worms in the garden means letting them be exactly as they are. We know how to do this: think of how we love other people. When you love another person, you love them as they are. You open yourself up to them without forcing them to be who you want them to be. You let your defenses down and let them in, even if it scares you. Why not love the wild in you the same way?

Notes

Introduction

1. Philosopher's note: The philosophers reading this book might be expecting me to start by presenting my own theory of emotions, but I'll have to disappoint them (it won't be the first time or the last). Although I don't consciously align myself with any particular theory of emotions, my starting point relies on first-personal reflection about our emotional lives. My discussion here will no doubt betray some of my theoretical sympathies, which mostly lie with philosophers such as (in no particular order) Robert Solomon, A. O. Rorty, Michael Stocker, Jeffrie Murphy, David Pugmire, Patricia Greenspan, Peter Goldie, Robert Roberts, Jerome Neu, and Martha Nussbaum.
2. Anna Julia Cooper, *A Voice from the South*, ed. Charles Lemert and Esme Bahn (Lanham, MD: Rowman & Littlefield, 1998), p. 92.
3. *A Voice from the South*, p. 93.
4. Philosopher's note: I'm not arguing for a strict perceptual account of emotions here. I agree with some aspects of a perceptual account but not all of them. I'm drawing more closely on the epistemological function of emotions that, for example, Alison Jaggar and Marilyn Frye argue for, as well as Robert Solomon's arguments about emotions and world-engagement. See Alison Jaggar "Love and Knowledge: Emotion in Feminist Epistemology" *Inquiry* 32, no. 2 (1989): 151–176; Marilyn Frye, "A Note on Anger," in *The Politics of Reality: Essays in Feminist Theory* (Trumansburg, NY: Crossing Press, 1983), and Robert C. Solomon, *True to Our Feelings: What Our Emotions Are Really Telling Us* (New York: Oxford University Press, 2007).
5. Philosopher's note: I'm indebted to Nomy Arpaly's work on acting against your best judgment in this section. See Nomy Arpaly, "On Rationally Acting against One's Best Judgment," *Ethics* 110 (2000): 488–513.
6. Krista K. Thomason, *Naked: The Dark Side of Shame and Moral Life* (New York: Oxford University Press, 2018), pp. 145–147.

7. Philosopher's note: Obviously Romanticism is a complex movement. Romanticism in the UK, for example, doesn't necessarily look like Romanticism in Germany. I have quite a bit of sympathy with some of their arguments. Some scholars of Romanticism will dispute parts of the description I give here, and that is fair. They can complain to me next time I see them at a conference. Solomon makes this connection between the Romantics and contemporary "reason versus emotion" claims. See Robert Solomon, *The Passions* (Indianapolis, IN: Hackett Publishing, 1993), pp. 52–66.

8. William Wordsworth, "Observations Prefixed to Lyrical Ballads," in *Classic Writings on Poetry*, ed. William Harmon, pp. 279–296 (Ithaca, NY: Columbia University Press, 2005), p. 281.

9. "Observations," p. 288.

10. Philosopher's note: The work of Robert Solomon and Michael Stocker is particularly prevalent in this section.

11. *The Passions*, p. 58.

12. Although people will usually say "Just the facts, ma'am," it turns out Friday never uses this phrase.

13. Philosopher's note: This is what Spelman calls "the Dumb View" of emotions. See Elizabeth V. Spelman, "Anger and Insubordination," in *Women, Knowledge, and Reality: Explorations in Feminist Philosophy*, pp. 263–274, ed. Ann Garry and Marilyn Pearsall (Winchester, MA: Unwin Hyman, 1989), p. 265.

14. Aristotle, *De Anima*, translated by David Bolotin (Macon. GA: Mercer University Press, 2018), lines 403a30–403b, pp. 9–10.

15. Antonio Damasio, *Looking for Spinoza: Joy, Sorrow, and the Feeling Brain* (Orlando, FL: Harcourt Books, 2003), pp. 30–33.

16. Philosopher's note: Reductive explanations like this are not that common in philosophical literature, but they are fairly common in popular parlance about emotions. Particularly in self-help literature, you encounter explanations of emotions that treat them as "brain states." Many philosophers assume the starting point of emotions as natural objects in the world, which you can see in the work of, for example, Jesse Prinz, Nico Frijda, and Owen Flanagan. Accounts like these are naturalized but are not necessarily reductive.

17. William James, "The Sentiment of Rationality," in *The Will to Believe and Other Essays in Popular Philosophy* (Auckland, New Zealand: The Floating Press, 2010) (ebook), p. 95.

18. Philosopher's note: The definition of *endoxa* and Aristotle's use of dialectic is contested. There are all sorts of questions about the relationship between the two as well as when and where Aristotle uses them. My discussion here draws from Charlotte Witt, "Dialectic, Motion, and Perception in *De Anima*: Book I," in *Essays on Aristotle's De Anima*, eds. Martha C. Nussbaum and Amelie Rorty, pp. 169–183 (Oxford: Oxford University Press, 1992), p. 169.
19. Bertrand Russell, *The Scientific Outlook* (London: George Allen & Unwin Ltd., 1931), p. 277.
20. A. M. Abdualkader et al., "Leech Therapeutic Applications," *Indian Journal of Pharmaceutical Sciences*, 75, no. 2 (2013): 127–137.
21. Interview in *Life* magazine, May 24, 1963.
22. The biographical information in the next few paragraphs comes from Sarah Bakewell, *How to Live or A Life of Montaigne in One Question and Twenty Attempts at an Answer* (New York: Other Press, 2010), Phillipe Desan, *Montaigne: A Life* (Princeton, NJ: Princeton University Press, 2017) and the introduction of Screech's translation of the *Essays*; see Michel de Montaigne, *The Complete Essays*, trans. by M. A. Screech (New York: Penguin Random House, 2003).
23. *The Complete Essays*, I:26, p. 180.
24. *The Complete Essays*, I:26, p. 181.
25. *The Complete Essays*, p. lxiii.

Chapter 1

1. George Orwell, "Reflections on Gandhi," in *A Collection of Essays* (New York: Doubleday Press, 1954), p. 177. This essay is referenced in a footnote in Susan Wolf, "Moral Saints," *The Journal of Philosophy* 79, no. 8 (1982): 419–439, p. 436.
2. Rajmohan Gandhi, *Gandhi: The Man, His People, and the Empire* (Berkeley: University of California Press, 2007), pp. 153–154.
3. *Mahatma Gandhi, An Autobiography: The Story of My Experience with Truth* (Boston, MA: Beacon Press, 1957), p. 317.
4. "Reflections on Gandhi," p. 183.
5. "Reflections on Gandhi," p. 182.
6. Philosopher's note: In addition to Wolf's "Moral Saints," my discussion in the following paragraphs is drawing on the following works: Bernard Williams, *Ethics and the Limits of Philosophy* (Cambridge, MA: Harvard University Press, 1985); Susan Wolf, *The Variety of Values: Essays on*

Morality, Meaning, and Love (New York: Oxford University Press, 2015); Cheshire Calhoun, *Doing Valuable Time: The Present, The Future, and a Meaningful Life* (New York: Oxford University Press, 2018).

7. Philosopher's note: I'm specifically drawing on Wolf's discussion of meaning here, see Susan Wolf, "Meaning and Morality" in *The Variety of Values*, pp. 127–140.

8. Jacob Rosenberg, "Why Silicon Valley Fell in Love with an Ancient Philosophy of Austerity," *Mother Jones*, January/February 2020, https://www.motherjones.com/media/2020/01/silicon-valley-stoicism-holiday.

9. Nancy Sherman, *Stoic Wisdom: Ancient Lessons for Modern Resilience* (New York: Oxford University Press, 2021), pp. 155–156.

10. For a detailed discussion of this phenomenon, see Joseph M. Reagle, *Hacking Life: Systemized Living and Its Discontents* (Cambridge, MA: MIT Press, 2019), especially Chapter 8.

11. Evan Thompson, *Why I Am Not a Buddhist* (New Haven, CT: Yale University Press, 2020), p. 118.

12. Charlotte Lieberman, "What Wellness Programs Won't Do for Workers," *Harvard Business Review*, August 14, 2019, https://hbr.org/2019/08/what-wellness-programs-dont-do-for-workers.

13. *Why I Am Not a Buddhist*, pp. 121–123.

14. See the EBT website for these descriptions: https://www.ebtconnect.net.

15. Peter Adamson, *Philosophy in the Hellenistic and Roman Worlds* (New York: Oxford University Press, 2015), p. 52.

16. A. A. Long and D. N. Sedley, *The Hellenistic Philosophers, Vol. 1* (New York: Cambridge University Press, 1987), pp. 2–3.

17. Philosopher's note: No doubt there are many aspects of my account of Stoicism that are subject to dispute. As will become clearer later, some of my own views have some things in common with aspects of Stoicism. What I'm providing here is at least one plausible interpretation of the basics of Stoicism, even if it's not without controversy. You can come complain to me at a conference, but the Romanticism scholars are ahead of you in line.

18. Simo Knuuttila, *Emotions in Ancient and Medieval Philosophy* (New York: Oxford University Press, 2004), pp. 47–49.

19. *Philosophy in the Hellenistic and Roman Worlds*, pp. 66–67.

20. *Philosophy in the Hellenistic and Roman Worlds*, pp. 68–69; Margaret Graver, *Stoicism and Emotion* (Chicago: University of Chicago Press, 2007), pp. 50–51.

21. *Stoicism and Emotion*, p. 2.

22. *Stoicism and Emotion*, pp. 39–41.

23. For discussion of the differences between Stoic views, see Richard Sorabji, *Emotion and Peace of Mind: From Stoic Agitation to Christian Temptation* (New York: Oxford University Press, 2000).

24. *Stoicism and Emotion*, p. 48; Martha C. Nussbaum, *Therapy of Desire: Theory and Practice in Hellenistic Ethics* (Princeton, NJ: Princeton University Press, 1994), p. 366.

25. *Emotion and Stoicism*, p. 55; *Emotion and Peace of Mind*, pp. 169–170; *Therapy of Desire*, p. 361.

26. Epictetus, *Discourses*, in *How to Be Free: An Ancient Guide to the Stoic Life*, trans. Anthony Long (Princeton, NJ: Princeton University Press, 2018), Book 4.1, lines 54–60, p. 113.

27. *Discourses*, Book 4.1, lines 64–80, pp. 117–123.

28. Epictetus, *The Encheiridion*, in *How to Be Free: An Ancient Guide to the Stoic Life*, trans. Anthony Long (Princeton, NJ: Princeton University Press, 2018), Book I.3, p. 9.

29. Philosopher's note: Some Stoics argue for *eupatheia* or "good *pathē*." It's fair to say that the sage seems to feel some sort of joy. That's fine, but I think it's false to conclude from this that the sage has anything like a normal emotional life.

30. *Emotion and Peace of Mind*, pp. 169–173.

31. The biographical information in this section is drawn from *Autobiography*, *The Man, His People, and the Empire* and Veena R. Howard, *Gandhi's Ascetic Activism: Renunciation and Social Action* (Albany: State University of New York Press, 2013).

32. Richard Davis, *The Bhagavad Gita: A Biography* (Princeton, NJ: Princeton University Press, 2015), pp. 6–12.

33. *The Bhagavad Gita*, 3rd edition, translated by Winthrop Sargeant and ed. Christopher Chapple (Albany: State University of New York Press, 2009), Book I, 34, p. 72.

34. Book I, 37; p. 75.

35. Philosopher's note: Gandhi's reading of the Gita is in some ways idiosyncratic. See *Autobiography*, pp. 66–68; *Gandhi's Ascetic Activism*, pp. 43–46.

36. Mahatma Gandhi, *The Bhagavad Gita According to Gandhi* (New Delhi: Orient Publishing, 2014), pp. 21–22.

37. *According to Gandhi*, pp. 14–15.

38. *According to Gandhi*, pp. 37–41.

39. Philosopher's note: Gandhi's reading of the Gita on emotions is not without controversy. For different perspectives, see Kathryn Ann Johnson,

"The Social Construction of Emotions in the Bhagavad Gita," *Journal of Religious Ethics* 35, no. 4 (2007): 655–679 and Purushottama Bilimoria, "Ethics of Emotion: Some Indian Reflections," in *Emotions in Asian Thought: A Dialogue in Comparative Philosophy*, ed. Joel Marks and Roger Ames (Albany, NY: SUNY Press, 1995).

40. *The Bhagavad Gita*, Book II, 56, p. 141; Book II, 58, p. 143; Book II, 62–63, pp. 147–148.
41. *The Bhagavad Gita*, Book II, 14, p. 99.
42. *According to Gandhi*, p. 34.
43. *According to Gandhi*, p. 39.
44. *According to Gandhi*, pp. 54–55.
45. *True to Our Feelings*, pp. 180–182.
46. *According to Gandhi*, p. 33.
47. Philosopher's note: Eliot was very knowledgeable about Spinoza (she translated some of his work). Given the influence of the Stoics on Spinoza, I think she sees emotional sainthood in him.
48. Philosopher's note: Indeed, some of the Roman Stoics in particular were less keen on emphasizing their cosmology. You might think Cicero and Seneca fall into the category.
49. For a chronicle of the positivity movement, see Barbara Ehrenreich, *Bright-Sided: How the Relentless Promotion of Positive Thinking Has Undermined America* (New York: Metropolitan Books, 2009).
50. For a history of the prosperity gospel, see Kate Bowler, *Blessed: A History of the American Prosperity Gospel* (New York: Oxford University Press, 2013).
51. Rhonda Byrne, *The Secret* (New York: Atria Books, 2006), p. 4.
52. Katie O'Malley, "How to Manifest: A Guide to Willing Your Goals into Existence in 2023," *Elle*, 5 January 2023, https://www.elle.com/uk/life-and-culture/culture/a38802302/how-to-manifest/ .
53. Todd Kashdan and Robert Biswas-Diener, *The Upside of Your Darkside* (New York: Hudson Street Press, 2014), p. 24.
54. I'm drawing on a point I made in one of my earlier papers, "Forgiveness or Fairness?" *Philosophical Papers* 44, no. 2 (2015): 233–260.

Chapter 2

1. All of this is recounted in Richard Scarry, *The Adventures of Lowly Worm* (New York: Sterling Press, 1995).

2. J. J. Gross, one of the pioneers of the field, has presented a good survey of the literature. See James J. Gross, "Emotion Regulation: Current Status and Future Prospects," *Psychological Inquiry* 26, no. 1 (2015): 1–26.

3. Nancy Sherman, *Making a Necessity of Virtue: Aristotle and Kant on Virtue* (New York: Cambridge University Press, 1997), p. 170.

4. For a review of this research, see A. M. Wood, J. J. Froh, and A. W. Geraghty, "Gratitude and Well-Being: A Review and Theoretical Integration," *Clinical Psychology Review* 30, no. 7 (2010): 890–905.

5. The biographical and background information in the following paragraphs is drawn from Confucius, *Analects*, trans. Edward Slingerland (Indianapolis, IN: Hackett Publishing, 2003); Philip Ivanhoe, *Confucian Moral Self-Cultivation* (Indianapolis, IN: Hackett Publishing, 2000) and *Confucian Reflections: Ancient Wisdom for Modern Times* (New York: Routledge, 2013); and Curie Virág, *The Emotions in Early Chinese Philosophy* (New York: Oxford University Press, 2017).

6. *Analects*, xxi.

7. The confusion between Daoism and Confucianism is made worse by the fact that Confucius appears as a character in some Daoist writings. For more on the history of the differences between Confucianism and Daoism, see David Shepherd Nivison, "The Classical Philosophical Writings," in *The Cambridge History of Ancient China: From Origins of Civilization to 221 BC*, ed. Michal Loewe and Edward Shaughnessy, pp. 745–812 (Cambridge: Cambridge University Press, 1999).

8. Philosopher's note: I'm drawing this list from Kwong-loi Shun, "Ren and Li in the Analects," in *Confucius and the Analects: New Essays*, ed. Bryan van Norden, pp. 53–72 (New York: Oxford University Press, 2002); Hagop Sarkissian, "Ritual and Rightness in the Analects," in *Dao Companion to the Analects*, ed. Amy Olberding, pp. 95–116 (New York: Springer, 2014); and Amy Olberding, *The Wrong of Rudeness: Learning Modern Civility from Ancient Chinese Philosophy* (New York: Oxford University Press, 2019), especially Chapters 5 and 6.

9. *Analects*, 2.5, p. 9 and 5.18, p. 46.

10. Philosopher's note: There is quite a bit of debate about exactly how *li* is supposed to be related to self-cultivation. Kwong-loi Shun, for example, identifies both an instrumentalist interpretation and a definitionalist interpretation ("Ren and Li," p. 56). Philip Ivanhoe argues for what he calls an "acquisition model" (*Confucian Moral Self-Cultivation*, p. 2). My reading here is indebted to Virág's discussion (*Emotions in Chinese Philosophy*, pp. 32–37).

11. Philosopher's note: I am relying on Slingerland's translation for both *wu-wei* and *ning* (*Analects*, Appendix 1, pp. 238–243).

12. *Analects*, 4.3, p. 30.

13. *Analects*, 11.21, p. 119.

14. *Analects*, 11.9, p. 114.

15. *Analects*, 11.10, p. 114.

16. The biographical information in this paragraph comes from Aristotle, *Nicomachean Ethics*, trans. Christopher Rowe with commentary by Sarah Broadie (New York: Oxford University Press, 2002) and Aristotle, *Rhetoric*, trans. George A. Kennedy (New York: Oxford University Press, 2007).

17. Philosopher's note: *Eudaimonia* requires other things besides self-cultivation (e.g., external goods), which is one of the things that separates Aristotle from the Stoics. Thanks to Aaron Harper for asking me about this.

18. *Nicomachean Ethics*, II.1, line 1103a15, p. 111.

19. *Nicomachean Ethics*, II.1, line 1103a18, p. 111.

20. *Nicomachean Ethics*, II.1, lines 1103b14–26, pp. 111–112.

21. *Nicomachean Ethics*, IV.5, lines 1125b27–b31, p. 152.

22. *Rhetoric*, II.2, lines 1378a36–38, p. 116.

23. *Nicomachean Ethics*, IV.5, lines 1126a5–a9, pp. 152–153.

24. Philosopher's note: There are some contentious issues about how to read the discussion of emotions in the *Rhetoric* and the *Nicomachean Ethics* together. They aren't central to the points I'm making here, but for more, see *Therapy of Desire*, Chapter 3; *Emotions in Ancient and Medieval Philosophy*, Chapter 1.4; Anthony Price, "Emotions in Plato and Aristotle," in *Oxford Handbook of Philosophy of Emotions*, ed. Peter Goldie, pp. 121–142 (New York: Oxford University Press, 2010). Jamie Dow "Aristotle's Theory of Emotions: Emotions as Pleasures and Pains," in *Moral Psychology and Human Action in Aristotle*, ed. Michael Pakaluk and Giles Pearson (New York: Oxford University Press, 2011), pp. 47–74.

25. *Nicomachean Ethics*, VI.5, pp. 179–180.

26. *Analects*, 4.17, p. 35.

27. Envy arises from malice in *Rhetoric*, 2.8, line 1387a, p, 142. Aristotle claims that malice is bad from the start in *Nicomachean Ethics*, II.6, line 1107a10–11, p. 117.

28. I will go to my grave grateful to Gregory Pappas for introducing me to this essay. It has become one of my favorite pieces of philosophy.

29. Dinitia Smith "A Utopia Awakens and Shakes Itself; Chautauqua, Once a Have for Religion Teachers, Survives," *The New York Times*, August 17,

1998, https://www.nytimes.com/1998/08/17/arts/utopia-awakens-sha kes-itself-chautauqua-once-cultural-haven-for-religion.html.

30. William James, *Talks to Teachers on Psychology* (Cambridge, MA: Harvard University Press, 1983), p. 152.

31. *Talks to Teachers*, p. 152.

32. *Talks to Teachers*, pp. 152–153.

33. W. E. B. Du Bois, *The Souls of Black Folk* (New York: W. W. Norton, 1903), p. 132.

34. *Souls*, p. 133.

35. *Souls*, p. 133.

36. *Souls*, p. 134.

37. Philosopher's note: My thinking here is drawing on "Love and Knowledge," "On Rationally Acting against One's Best Judgment," and David Pugmire, *Rediscovering Emotion* (Edinburgh: Edinburgh University Press, 1998) (especially Chapter 8).

38. For an extended discussion of the emotional complexity of grief, see Michael Cholbi, *Grief: A Philosophical Guide* (Princeton, NJ: Princeton University Press, 2021).

39. Aaron Ben-Ze'ev and Ruhama Goussinsky, *In the Name of Love: Romantic Ideology and Its Victims* (New York: Oxford University Press, 2008), p. 2.

40. *In the Name of Love*, p. 4.

41. For examples and an extensive discussion of the downsides of love, see *In the Name of Love*, Chapter 3.

42. Bill Hicks, *Love All the People* (Berkeley, CA: Soft Skull Press, 2008), p. 249.

43. Bill Hicks might have been self-destructive: he struggled with alcohol, but it's not clear that his addiction was caused by his anger.

44. I thought I had coined this term, which I took to be a twist on "mental hygiene" from Norvin Richards, "Forgiveness," *Ethics* 99, no. 1 (1988): 77–97, p. 79. I have since learned that apparently the Dalai Lama coined it in a speech on 29 August 2016, see "Education on emotional hygiene is in great need: Dalai Lama," https://www.dalailama.com/news/2016/education-on-emotional-hygiene-is-in-great-need-dalai-lama

45. Philosopher's note: Philosophers of emotion talk about this in terms of "negative valence" (negative emotions feel bad). The notion of valence frankly distorts more than it clarifies. Solomon explains the problems with valence in *True to Our Feelings*, Chapter 15.

46. For skepticism about this literature, see *Bright-Sided*, pp. 155–172.

47. *The Upside of Your Dark Side*, pp. 97–98.

48. *The Upside of Your Dark Side*, pp. 101–105.

49. *The Upside of Your Dark Side*, pp. 69–72.
50. Daniel Goleman, *Emotional Intelligence: Why It Can Matter More than IQ* (London: Bloomsbury, 1995), p. 6.
51. Deena Skolnick Weisberg, Frank C. Keil, Joshua Goodstein, Elizabeth Rawson, and Jeremy R. Gray, "The Seductive Allure of Neuroscience Explanations," *Journal of Cognitive Neuroscience* 20, no. 3 (2008): 470–477.
52. Philosopher's note: For more on the challenges of making evolutionary arguments about human psychology, see Subrena Smith, "Is Evolutionary Psychology Possible?" *Biological Theory* 15 (2020): 39–49.

Chapter 3

1. The summary of Darwin's work and facts about earthworms in this paragraph come from *The Earth Moved: On the Remarkable Achievements of Earth Worms* (Chapel Hill, NC: Algonquin Books, 2004).
2. Charles Darwin, *The Formation of Vegetable Mould*, *The Works of Charles Darwin*, Vol. 28, ed. Paul H. Barrett and R. B. Freeman (London: William Pickering, 1989), p. 14.
3. *The Formation of Vegetable Mould*, pp. 29–40.
4. *The Formation of Vegetable Mould*, p. 43.
5. *The Formation of Vegetable Mould*, p. 139.
6. For overviews of the extensive literature on Satan in Milton, see Neil Forsyth, *The Satanic Epic* (Princeton, NJ: Princeton University Press, 2003), pp. 64–76.
7. John Milton, *Paradise Lost*, ed. Gordon (Teskey, NY: W. W. Norton, 2020), 1.34–37, p. 6.
8. *Paradise Lost* 5.662–665, p. 128.
9. *Paradise Lost*, 1.601–603, p. 22.
10. *Paradise Lost*, 1.605, p. 22.
11. *Paradise Lost*, 1.620, p. 23.
12. *Paradise Lost*, 4.66–83, p. 82.
13. *Paradise Lost*, 4.114–115, p. 83,
14. *Paradise Lost*, 4.506–508, p. 94,
15. *Paradise Lost*, 5.790–796, pp. 131–132,
16. This interpretation of Satan is drawn from William Hazlitt's reading, in which Satan is "self-will personified." See William Hazlitt, *Lectures on English Poets*, "Of Milton and Shakespeare" (Philadelphia: Thomas Dobson and Son, 1818) (ebook).
17. *Paradise Lost*, 1.263, p. 12.

18. Philosopher's note: I'm drawing on discussions of self-love and self-interest from Susan Wolf, Harry Frankfurt, and bell hooks. See Susan Wolf, "Morality and the View from Here," in *The Variety of Values*: Harry Frankfurt, *The Reasons of Love* (Princeton, NJ: Princeton University Press, 2004), especially Chapter 3; and bell hooks, *All About Love: New Visions* (New York: William Morrow, 2018), especially Chapter 7. My use of attachment is drawing on Monique Wonderly, "On Being Attached," *Philosophical Studies* 173 (2016): 223–244.

19. Philosopher's note: Solomon thinks this is to some extent true of all emotions; see *The Passions*, pp. 128–130. Jeffrie Murphy presents something like this idea in his discussion of resentment. He writes that resentment operates "in defense . . . of certain values of the self." He means self-respect in the moral sense, but the "values of the self" that I'm appealing to are not so specific. See Jeffrie Murphy and Jean Hampton, *Forgiveness and Mercy* (New York: Oxford University Press, 1988), p. 16.

20. Philosopher's note: Buddhist philosophers have a variety of views about negative emotions. For arguments that some Buddhists don't reject strong emotions, see Emily McRae, "A Passionate Buddhist Life," *The Journal of Religious Ethics* 40, no. 1 (2012): 99–121.

21. Philosopher's note: One source of disagreement is about exactly how Buddhist views of truth relate to their ethical practice. See The Cowherds, *Moonpaths: Ethics and Emptiness* (New York: Oxford University Press, 2016), especially Chapters 5, 7, and 11.

22. *Moonpaths*, p. 2.

23. Nicolas Bommarito, *Seeing Clearly: A Buddhist Guide to Life* (New York: Oxford University Press, 2020), p. 13.

24. *Moonpaths*, p. 2.

25. *Moonpaths*, pp. 47–48; *Seeing Clearly*, pp. 93–95.

26. Some schools of Buddhism accept the existence of a self, the Nyāya, for example.

27. Philosopher's note: For a more detailed explanation of the difference between selves and persons in Buddhism, see Mark Siderits, *How Things Are: An Introduction to Buddhist Metaphysics* (New York: Oxford University Press, 2022), Chapters 2 and 3.

28. Nāgājuna, *Rātnavalī*, in *Buddhist Advice for Living and Liberation*, trans. by Jeffery Hopkins (Ithaca, NY: Snow Lion Press, 1998, I.29), p. 97.

29. *Rātnavalī*, III.271, p. 129.

30. Philosopher's note: For just a handful of examples, see Derek Parfit, *Reasons and Persons* (New York: Oxford University Press, 1984); Iris

Murdoch, *The Sovereignty of the Good* (New York: Routledge, 2001); Owen Flanagan, *The Bodhisattva's Brain* (Cambridge, MA: MIT Press, 2011).

31. *Sovereignty of the Good*, p. 51.

32. *Sovereignty of the Good*, p. 66.

33. Philosopher's note: This problem is more pronounced for the non-Mahāyāna Buddhists. Since Mahāyāna Buddhists believe that their practitioners must remain in the birth–death cycle as long as there are suffering beings in the world, they shouldn't withdraw from their fellows. Buddhist philosophers have wrestled with the connection between compassion and the no-self; see *Moonpaths*, Chapters 5 and 6.

34. The biographical details are drawn from the timeline in Friedrich Nietzsche, *The Gay Science*, trans. Josefine Naukoff and Adrian del Caro (Cambridge: Cambridge University Press, 2001), pp. xxiii–xxv.

35. Julian Young, *Friedrich Nietzsche: A Philosophical Biography* (New York: Cambridge University Press, 2010), pp. 363–364.

36. *Friedrich Nietzsche*, pp. 554–558.

37. Philosopher's note: I am echoing the reading of Nietzsche and Montaigne from Robert Pippin, *Nietzsche, Psychology, and First Philosophy* (Chicago: University of Chicago Press, 2010) and R. Lanier Anderson and Rachel Cristy, "What Is 'The Meaning of Our Cheerfulness'? Philosophy as a Way of Life in Nietzsche and Montaigne," *European Journal of Philosophy* 25, no. 4 (2017): 1514–1549.

38. Friedrich Nietzsche, *Schopenhauer as Educator*, in *Untimely Mediations*, ed. David Breazeale and trans. R. J. Hollingdale (Cambridge: Cambridge University Press, 1997), section 2, p. 135.

39. Nietzsche, *Schopenhauer as Educator*, p. 135.

40. Philosopher's note: I'm reading The Saint as one of Nietzsche's "types," as Mark Alfano calls them. See Mark Alfano, *Nietzsche's Moral Psychology* (Cambridge: Cambridge University Press, 2019), pp. 55–56. I'm using the word "saint" to match the language from early works such as *The Birth of Tragedy, Human, All Too Human*, and *The Gay Science*, but in the later works, this figure is more identified with the priestly type. Thanks to Aaron Harper for pressing me on this.

41. Friedrich Nietzsche, *Human, All Too Human*, trans. R.J. Hollingdale (Cambridge: Cambridge University Press, 1996), I.1.27, p. 26.

42. *Human, All Too Human*, I.3.141, pp. 75–76.

43. *Human, All Too Human*, I.3.137, p. 74.

44. *Human, All Too Human*, I.3.133, p. 71.

45. Philosopher's note: There is some controversy over exactly how to under-stand Nietzsche's own conception of the self. For a helpful discussion, see Sebastian Gardner, "Nietzsche, the Self, and the Disunity of Philosophical Reason," in *Nietzsche on Freedom and Autonomy*, ed. Ken Gemes and Simon May (New York: Oxford University Press, 2009).

46. Philosopher's note: Nietzsche describes the philosophical development of divorcing the "real world" from the "illusory world" in *Twilight of the Idols*, "How the 'True World' Finally Became a Fable." See Friedrich Nietzsche, *The Anti-Christ, Ecce Homo, Twilight of the Idols*, ed. Aaron Ridley and trans. Judith Norman (Cambridge: Cambridge University Press, 2005), p. 171.

47. Philosopher's note: This section is drawing on arguments from Robert C. Solomon, *Living with Nietzsche: What the Great "Immoralist" Has to Teach Us* (New York: Oxford University Press, 2004), especially Chapter Three, and Aaron Harper, "Playing, Valuing, and Living: Examining Nietzsche's Playful Response to Nihilism," *Journal of Value Inquiry* 50 (2016): 305–323.

48. For a detailed exploration of the relationship between nihilism and the emotions, see Kaitlyn Creasy, *The Problem of Affective Nihilism in Nietzsche* (New York: Palgrave-Macmillan, 2020).

49. *Gay Science* IV.276, p. 157.

50. *Gay Science* IV.290, p. 164.

51. Philosopher's note: My discussion here draws on Owen's reconstruction of Nietzsche's self-love; see David Owen, "Autonomy, Self-Respect, and Self-Love: Nietzsche on Ethical Agency," in *Nietzsche on Freedom and Autonomy*, ed. Ken Gemes and Simon May (New York: Oxford University Press, 2009).

52. Clinical psychology advocates a similar kind of acceptance: we should "make room" for them with an "attitude of genuine curiosity and self-compassion." See Steven C. Hayes, Kirk D. Strosahl, and Kelly G. Wilson, *Acceptance and Commitment Therapy: The Process of and Practice of Mindful Change* (second edition) (New York: Guilford Press, 2012), pp. 65–66.

53. *Gay Science*, IV.334, p. 186.

54. *Gay Science*, V.382.

55. I've argued for this in more detail in *Naked*, pp. 118–121.

56. Philosopher's note: Psychologists sometimes call this "emotional literacy" or "emotional granularity." See Lisa Feldman Barrett, *How Emotions Are Made: The Secret Life of the Brain* (New York: Houghton Mifflin Harcourt,

2017), pp. 180–183 and Claude Steiner, *Achieving Emotional Literacy* (New York: Avon Books, 1997).

Chapter 4

1. W. E. B. Du Bois, "The Shape of Fear," *The North American Review* 223 (1926): 291–304, p. 291.
2. "Shape of Fear," pp. 292–293.
3. "Shape of Fear," p. 294.
4. "Shape of Fear," p. 302.
5. The biographical information in this paragraph is taken from Seneca, *Anger, Mercy, Revenge*, trans. Robert A. Kaster and Martha Nussbaum (Chicago: University of Chicago Press, 2010), pp. vii–ix.
6. *Anger, Mercy, Revenge*, p. 14.
7. *Anger, Mercy, Revenge*, p. 14.
8. *Anger, Mercy, Revenge*, p. 15.
9. *Anger, Mercy, Revenge*, p. 16.
10. *Anger, Mercy, Revenge*, p. 16.
11. *Anger, Mercy, Revenge*, p. 19.
12. *Anger, Mercy, Revenge*, p. 21.
13. *Anger, Mercy, Revenge*, pp. 23–24.
14. *Anger, Mercy, Revenge*, p. 25.
15. Biographical details in the paragraph are taken from Śāntideva, *A Guide to the Bodhisattva's Way of Life*, trans. Vensa A. Wallace and B. Alan Wallace (Ithaca, NY: Snow Lion Press, 1997), pp. 11–13.
16. These details are from Tāranātha's history of Buddhism, dated around the 16th or 17th century (*Bodhisattva's Way of Life*, pp. 11–12).
17. *Moonpaths*, p. 16.
18. *Bodhisattva's Way of Life*, 4.47, p. 44.
19. *Bodhisattva's Way of Life*, 6.8, p. 62.
20. *Bodhisattva's Way of Life*, 6.22, p. 64.
21. *Bodhisattva's Way of Life*, 6.33, p. 65.
22. *Bodhisattva's Way of Life*, 6.44, p. 67.
23. *Bodhisattva's Way of Life*, 6.52, p. 67.
24. Philosopher's note: For a more extended discussion of Audre Lorde's conception of anger, see Myisha Cherry, *The Case for Rage: Why Anger Is Essential to Anti-Racist Struggle* (New York: Oxford University Press, 2021).
25. "A Note on Anger," p. 85.

26. "A Note on Anger," p. 89.

27. Audre Lorde, "The Uses of Anger: Women Responding to Racism," in *Sister Outsider* (Berkeley, CA: Crossing Press, 1984), p. 125 and "A Note on Anger," pp. 84–85.

28. "Uses of Anger," p. 124.

29. "Uses of Anger," p. 124.

30. "Uses of Anger," p. 127.

31. "Uses of Anger," p. 128.

32. "Uses of Anger," p. 131.

33. Owen Flanagan, *How to Do Things with Emotions: The Morality of Anger and Shame Across Cultures* (Princeton, NJ: Princeton University Press, 2021), p. 46. Flanagan thinks of pain-passing as a type of anger. I think of it as just a coping mechanism for anger.

34. *Case for Rage*, pp. 153–154.

35. Philosopher's note: Cherry talks about anger policing as well, but her definition is different from mine. In her view, anger police are insincere in their evaluations and think anger is inappropriate by its mere presence. I agree this is often the case, though I also think there are sincere anger police who just think that the reasons for being "rightfully" angry are too few. Myisha Cherry, "The Errors and Limitations of Our Anger-Evaluating Ways," in *The Moral Psychology of Anger*, ed. Myisha Cherry and Owen Flanagan (Lanham, MD: Rowman & Littlefield, 2017), pp. 57–61.

36. I've argued for this in more detail in "How Should We Feel about Recalcitrant Emotions?" in *Self-Blame and Moral Responsibility*, ed. Andreas Brekke Carlsson (Cambridge: Cambridge University Press, 2022), pp. 134–148.

37. Philosopher's note: I'm drawing here on Solomon's discussion of the subjectivity of emotions in *The Passions*, pp. 115–117.

38. "Note on Anger," p. 87.

39. Philosopher's note: Martha Nussbaum argues that we should feel "transitional anger" about injustices in her *Anger and Forgiveness: Resentment, Generosity, Justice* (New York: Oxford University Press, 2016), pp. 35–37. Cherry defends "Lordean rage" (inspired by Lorde's account of anger) in *The Case for Rage*, pp. 23–27. Flanagan allows for "loving anger" (*How to Do Things with Emotions*, pp. 59–62). Agnes Callard argues against these strategies of "purifying" anger in *On Anger* (Cambridge, MA: Boston Review Forum, 2020), pp. 21–25.

40. Philosopher's note: I think Lorde's views about anger are more complicated than this. She places value on emotional life that goes beyond its ability

to bring about social change. You see this viewpoint in her essay "Uses of the Erotic: The Erotic as Power" and in her interview with Adrienne Rich, both in *Sister Outsider*. For more detail, see Caleb Ward, "Feeling, Knowledge, Self-Preservation: Audre Lorde's Oppositional Agency and Some Implications for Ethics," *Journal of the American Philosophical Association* 6, no. 4 (2020): 463–482.

41. Philosopher's note: I have argued for this view in the past, though I no longer agree with it. See Krista K. Thomason "The Moral Necessity of Anger," in *The Ethics of Anger*, ed. Court D. Lewis and Gregory L. Bock (Lanham, MD: Rowman & Littlefield, 2020), pp. 83–102.

42. Philosopher's note: Philosophers who work on negative emotions often employ this strategy of dividing negative emotions into good and bad kinds, but I've argued against it; see Thomason, *Naked*, pp. 26–29.

43. James Baldwin, "Everybody's Protest Novel," in *James Baldwin: Collected Essays* (New York: Library of America, 1998), p. 15.

44. For a detailed discussion of the disagreement between Baldwin and Wright, see Maurice Charney, "James Baldwin's Quarrel with Richard Wright," *American Quarterly* 15, no. 1 (1963): 65–75.

45. "Protest Novel," p. 16.

46. "Protest Novel," p. 18.

47. Philosopher's note: Cherry has argued that Baldwin has an account of what she calls "Black rage," which is, as I read it, a form of righteous anger. I can't argue for this claim here, but I think her account does not quite grapple with Baldwin's criticism of Wright's work. I think that criticism has implications for Baldwin's moral psychology. See Myisha Cherry, "On James Baldwin and Black Rage," *Critical Philosophy of Race*, 10 (2022): 1–21.

48. Will Oremus, Chris Alacantara, James B. Merrill, and Arthur Galocha, "How Facebook Shapes Your Feed," *The Washington Post*, October 26, 2021, https://www.washingtonpost.com/technology/interactive/2021/how-facebook-algorithm-works.

49. Quoted in Kate Manne, *Down Girl: The Logic of Misogyny* (New York: Oxford University Press, 2018), p. 35.

50. *Down Girl*, pp. 35–36.

51. Background on incels and the manosphere in this paragraph is drawn from Talia Lavin, *Culture Warlords: My Journey into the Dark Web of White Supremacy* (New York: Hachette Books, 2020) and Laura Bates, *Men Who Hate Women: The Extremism Nobody Is Talking About* (London: Simon & Schuster, 2020).

52. *Men Who Hate Women*, pp. 354–435.

53. Both Lavin and Bates create fake online incel profiles based on stories like this one; see *Culture Warlords*, pp. 99–101 and *Men Who Hate Women*, pp. 11–13.

54. *Men Who Hate Women*, p. 13.

55. *Down Girl*, pp. 172–173.

56. Quoted in *Down Girl*, p. 174.

57. "Shape of Fear," p. 293.

58. "Shape of Fear," p. 294.

Chapter 5

1. Some of the material from this chapter draws on my earlier article, "The Moral Value of Envy," *Southern Journal of Philosophy* 53, no. 1 (2015): 36–53.

2. William Shakespeare, *Othello*, in *The Annotated Shakespeare* by Burton Raffel (New Haven, CT: Yale University Press, 2005), Act 3, Scene 3, p. 109.

3. Bridget K. Balint, "Envy in the Intellectual Discourse of the High Middle Ages," in *The Seven Deadly Sins: From Communities to Individuals*, ed. Richard Newhauser (Leiden, The Netherlands: Brill, 2007), p. 43.

4. J. R. C. Cousland, "The Much Suffering Eye in Antioch's House of the Evil Eye: Is It Mithraic?" *Religious Studies and Theology* 24, no.1 (2005): 61.

5. Ovid, *Metamorphoses*, trans. Frank Justus Miller, Loeb Classical Library (Cambridge, MA: Harvard University Press, 1977), Book II.764, pp. 112–113.

6. *Metamorphoses*, Book II.775–777, pp. 114–115.

7. Douglas P. Lackey, "Giotto in Pauda: A New Geography of the Human Soul," *Journal of Ethics* 9, no. 3/4 (2005): 551–572.

8. For a discussion of some of the literature that shows people's unwillingness to admit their jealousy and envy, see Sara Protasi, *The Philosophy of Envy* (New York: Cambridge University Press, 2021), pp. 26–28.

9. For a good discussion of the issues of distinguishing envy and jealousy, see Sara Protasi, "'I'm Not Envious, I'm Just Jealous!': On the Difference between Envy and Jealousy," *Journal for the American Philosophical Association* 3, no. 3 (2017): 316–333.

10. For a detailed discussion of Medea and jealousy, see Ed Sanders, *Envy and Jealousy in Classical Athens: A Socio-Psychological Approach* (New York: Oxford University Press, 2014), especially Chapter 8.

11. Euripides, "Medea," in *Euripides: Ten Plays*, trans. Paul Roche (New York: Signet Classic, 1998), p. 346. "Hell hath no fury like a woman

scorned" is actually a misquote of a line from the 1679 play *The Mourning Bride* by William Congreve.

12. Jerome Neu, *A Tear Is an Intellectual Thing: The Meanings of Emotion* (New York: Oxford University Press, 2000), p. 43.

13. The quotations and descriptions are taken from the documentary *Laurel Canyon: A Place in Time*, directed by Alison Ellwood, produced by Frank Marshall and Amblin Television, 2020.

14. Ben Ze'ev uses the term *three-party relation*. Aaron Ben-Ze'ev, *The Subtlety of Emotions* (Cambridge, MA: MIT Press, 2000), p. 289.

15. *Subtlety of Emotions*, p. 293; *A Tear Is an Intellectual Thing*, p. 45; *Philosophy of Envy*, p. 9.

16. For an overview of the older psychological literature on nonromantic jealousy, see Paul Davis and Robert Hill, "'Platonic Jealousy:' A Conceptualization and Review of the Literature on Non-Romantic Pathological Jealousy," *British Journal of Medical Psychology* 73 (2000): 505–517.

17. Philosopher's note: My discussion of love here is inspired by *A Tear Is an Intellectual Thing* and Robert Nozick, "Love's Bond" in *The Philosophy of (Erotic) Love*, ed. Robert C. Solomon and Kathleen M. Higgins, pp. 417–432 (Lawrence: University of Kansas Press, 1991).

18. Philosopher's note: I'm not staking out a position about whether love is irrational.

19. Philosopher's note: I'm partly drawing on Protasi's discussion of "wise love" in the case of envy; see *Philosophy of Envy*, pp. 111–112.

20. J. David Velleman makes this point: "Love disarms our emotional defenses; it makes us vulnerable to the other." See J. David Velleman, "Love as a Moral Emotion," *Ethics* 109 (1999): 338–375, p. 361.

21. "Love's Bond," p. 419.

22. Pope Gregory I, *Moralia in Job*, trans. John Henry Parker (London: J.G.F. and J. Rivington. 1844) (ebook provided by Lectionary Central), Book XXXI.xlv.87.

23. *Moralia*, Book XXXI.i.1.

24. *Moralia*, Book XXXI.xlv.88.

25. Background on Bacon and the *Essays* in this paragraph comes from the introductions of *The Cambridge Companion to Francis Bacon*, ed. Markku Peltonen (Cambridge: Cambridge University Press, 1996) and Francis Bacon, *Essays, or Counsel, Civil and Moral* in *The Oxford Francis Bacon*, Vol. XV, ed. Michael Kiernan (Oxford: Oxford University Press, 2000).

26. "Of Envy," IX.79, p. 29.

27. "Of Envy," IX.57, p. 28 and IX.31, p. 27.
28. "Of Envy," IX.37–38, p. 28.
29. "Of Envy," IX.80, p. 29.
30. "Of Envy," IX.40–41, p. 28.
31. "Of Envy," IX.95–96, p. 29.
32. "Of Envy," IX.137–139, p. 30.
33. "Of Envy," IX.145–146, p. 31.
34. "Of Envy," IX.169–170, p. 31.
35. "Of Envy," IX.173, p. 31.
36. Philosopher's note: These various criticisms of envy appear in: Robert C. Roberts, "What Is Wrong with Wicked Feelings?" *American Philosophical Quarterly 28* (1991): 17–18; Don Herzog, "Envy: Poisoning the Banquet They Cannot Taste," in *Wicked Pleasures: Meditations on the Seven "Deadly" Sins*, ed. Robert C. Solomon (Lanham, MD: Rowman & Littlefield, 1999), p. 143; Gabriele Taylor, *Deadly Vices* (New York: Oxford University Press, 2006), pp. 48–50; Susan T. Fiske, *Envy Up, Scorn Down: How Status Divides Us* (New York: Russell Sage Foundation, 2011), p. 95; Martha Nussbaum, *The Monarchy of Fear: A Philosopher Looks at Our Political Crisis* (New York: Simon & Schuster, 2018), pp. 136–138; *A Tear in an Intellectual Thing*, p. 49.
37. *Envy Up*, p. 24.
38. *Philosophy of Envy*, pp. 6–7.
39. Helmut Schoeck, *Envy: A Theory of Social Behavior* (Indianapolis, IN: Liberty Press, 1966), p. 33.
40. Philosopher's note: This beneficial kind of envy is sometimes called "emulative envy." For a detailed discussion of different accounts of emulative envy, see *Philosophy of Envy*, pp. 44–54.
41. Marguerite La Caze, "Envy and Resentment" *Philosophical Explorations 4*, no. 1 (2001): 35–36; Sianne Ngai, *Ugly Feelings* (Cambridge, MA: Harvard University Press, 2005), p. 130.
42. "Envy and Resentment," p. 37; Miriam Bankovsky, "Excusing Economic Envy: On Injustice and Impotence," *Journal of Applied Philosophy 35*, no. 2 (2018): 263; *Monarchy of Fear*, pp. 145–146; See *Philosophy of Envy*, Chapter 5, for a detailed discussion of political envy.
43. *Envy Up*, p. 104.
44. "Poisoning the Banquet," p. 141.
45. "Poisoning the Banquet," p. 142.
46. For example, Justin D'Arms and Alison Duncan Kerr, "Envy in the Philosophical Tradition," in *Envy, Theory and Research*, ed. Richard Smith,

pp. 39–59 (New York: Oxford University Press, 2008), pp. 45–48. For arguments against this view, see *Philosophy of Envy*, pp. 52–54.

47. *Philosophy of Envy*, Chapter 4.

48. "Poisoning the Banquet," p. 146.

Chapter 6

1. Some work in this chapter, including the Warner Bros. case, draws on my previous paper, "I'll Show You: Spite as a Reactive Attitude," *The Monist* 103 (2020): 163–175.

2. Details about the contentious relationship between Selzer and the animators are taken from Chuck Jones, *Chuck Amuck: The Life and Times of an Animated Cartoonist* (New York: Macmillan, 1989) and Tom Sito, *Drawing the Line: The Untold Story of the Animation Unions from Bosko to Bart Simpson* (Lexington: University of Kentucky Press, 2006).

3. Jonathan Metzl, *Dying of Whiteness: How the Politics of Racial Resentment is Killing America's Heartland* (New York: Basic Books, 2020), pp. 147–149.

4. *Dying of Whiteness*, p. 151.

5. *Dying of Whiteness*, pp. 171–183.

6. *Dying of Whiteness*, pp. 185–187.

7. Steven Nadler, *A Book Forged in Hell: Spinoza's Scandalous Treatise and the Birth of the Secular Age* (Princeton, NJ: Princeton University Press, 2011), p. 5.

8. Quoted in *A Book Forged in Hell*, pp. 7–8.

9. Baruch Spinoza, *Ethics*, in *The Collected Works of Spinoza, Vol. I*, ed. and trans. Edwin Curley (Princeton, NJ: Princeton University Press, 1985), Part IV, P73, p. 587.

10. *Ethics*, Part IV, Appendix §4, p. 588.

11. Philosopher's note: Spinozists will no doubt object to some of what I've said here. I am, for example, sidestepping the thorny question about the relationship between *Natura naraturans* and *Natura naturata*. You can come yell at me at a conference, but there are lots of people ahead you. I'm indebted to Garrett's and Lebuffe's work for help with some of my Spinoza reconstruction; see Don Garrett, *Necessity and Nature in Spinoza's Philosophy* (New York: Oxford University Press, 2018) and Michael Lebuffe, *From Bondage to Freedom: Spinoza on Human Excellence* (New York: Oxford University Press, 2009).

12. *Ethics*, Part I, Def. 3, p. 408.

13. Philosopher's note: Spinoza distinguishes between attributes and modes, but the details of that discussion aren't necessary for my purposes here.

14. *Ethics*, Part I, Def. 6, p. 409.

15. *Necessity and Nature*, p. 465; *From Bondage to Freedom*, pp. 33–34.

16. Philosopher's note: My reading here is drawing on Steven Nadler, "On Spinoza's 'Free Man,'" *Journal of the American Philosophical Association* 1, no. 1 (2015): 103–120.

17. *Ethics*, Part III, Def. 3, p. 493.

18. *Ethics*, Part III, P11, pp. 500–501.

19. Philosopher's note: This quotation is from *God, Man, and His Well-Being*. As Curley points out in the Preface, the lineage of this early work is hotly contested and was likely not intended for publication. *God, Man, and His Well-Being* in *The Collected Works of Spinoza, Vol. I*, Chapter XXVI, line 10930, p. 147.

20. *Ethics*, Part IV, P37, p. 565.

21. *Ethics*, Part IV, P46, pp. 572–573.

22. *Ethics*, Part IV, P45, p. 571–572.

23. *Ethics*, Part IV, P46, p. 573.

24. Portmann attributes a position like this to Baudelaire. See John Portmann, *When Bad Things Happen to Other People* (New York: Routledge, 2000), p. 40.

25. *When Bad Things Happen to Other People*, pp. 32–34; James McNamee, "Schadenfreude in Sport: Envy, Justice, and Self-Esteem," *Journal of the Philosophy of Sport* 30, no. 1 (2003): 1–16, pp. 8–11.

26. *When Bad Things Happen*, pp. 35–39; *The Subtlety of Emotions*, pp. 356–357.

27. Richard H. Smith, *The Joy of Pain: Schadenfreude and the Dark Side of Human Nature* (New York: Oxford University Press, 2013), p. 71.

28. *When Bad Things Happen*, p. 57.

29. Philosopher's note: Portmann attributes to Nietzsche the link between human folly and humor. I agree with this reading and would wager Nietzsche develops it in part because of his admiration for Montaigne; see *When Bad Things Happen*, pp. 127–128.

30. *Essays*, I.31, p. 228, introductory note.

31. *Essays*, 1.31, p. 231.

32. *Essays*, 1.31, p. 233.

33. *Essays*, 1.31, p. 235.

34. *Essays*, 1.31, p. 236.

35. *Essays*, 1.31, p. 241.

36. *Essays*, 2.15, p. 695.
37. *Essays*, 2.15, p. 695.
38. Essays, 3.11, p. 1165.
39. *Essays*, 2.15, p. 699.
40. *Essays*, 1.39, pp. 266–267.
41. *Essays*, 1.39, p. 268.
42. *Essays*, 1.39, p. 268.
43. *Essays*, 1.39, p. 269.
44. Essays, 1.39, p. 270.
45. Background on the civil wars in this paragraph comes from Ulrich Langer, "Montaigne's Political and Religious Context," in *The Cambridge Companion to Montaigne*, ed. Ulrich Langer (New York: Cambridge University Press, 2005).
46. *Essays*, 2.11, p. 484.
47. *Essays*, 2.5, p. 411.
48. *Essays*, 2.12, p. 495.
49. *Essays*, 2.12, p. 495.
50. Lilliana Mason, *Uncivil Agreement: How Politics Became Our Identity* (Chicago: University of Chicago Press, 2018), pp. 45–47.
51. *Uncivil Agreement*, p. 4.
52. For a summary of the cola wars, see Becky Little, "How the 'Blood Feud' between Coke and Pepsi Escalated during the 1980s Cola Wars," June 11, 2019, History.com, https://www.history.com/news/cola-wars-pepsi-new-coke-failure
53. *Joy of Pain*, p. 42.
54. *Uncivil Agreement*, pp. 9–14; *Joy of Pain*, pp. 34–35.
55. *Uncivil Agreement*, p. 9; *Joy of Pain*, pp. 35–36.
56. *Joy of Pain*, pp. 41–42.
57. *Uncivil Agreement*, p. 12.
58. For an example of a tribalism argument, see Joshua Greene, *Moral Tribes: Emotion, Reason, and the Gap Between Us and Them* (New York: Penguin, 2014).
59. *Uncivil Agreement*, p. 100.
60. For arguments about self-expression and bumper stickers, see Charles E. Chase, "Bumper Stickers and Car Signs Ideology and Identity," *Journal of Popular Culture* 26, no. 3 (1992): 107–119.
61. *Dying of Whiteness*, p. 288.
62. Arlie Hochschild, *Strangers in Their Own Land: Anger and Mourning of the American Right* (New York: The New Press, 2016), pp. 135–139.

Chapter 7

1. Jane Addams, "The Devil Baby at Hull-House," in *Radiant Truths: Essential Dispatches, Reports, Confessions, and Other Essays on American Belief*, ed. Jeff Sharlet (New Haven, CT: Yale University Press, 2014). The essay was originally published in *The Atlantic* in 1916.

2. "Devil Baby," p. 91.

3. "Devil Baby," p. 92.

4. "Devil Baby," p. 93.

5. "Devil Baby," p. 93.

6. Thomas Hill Jr., "Basic Respect and Cultural Diversity," in *Respect, Pluralism, and Justice: Kantian Perspectives* (New York: Oxford University Press, 2000), p. 60.

7. Background on Rousseau's life comes from Patrick Riley, "Introduction to the Life and Works of Jean-Jacques Rousseau," in *The Cambridge Companion to Rousseau*, ed. Patrick Riley, pp. 1–7 (New York: Cambridge University Press, 2001).

8. Philosopher's note: My thinking about *amour-propre* is influenced by Niko Kolodny, "The Explanation of Amour-Propre," *Philosophical Review* 119, no. 2 (2010): 165–200.

9. Jean-Jacques Rousseau, "Discourse on the Origins and Foundations of Inequality among Men," in *The Basic Political Writings*, second edition, trans. and ed. Donald A. Cress (Indianapolis, IN: Hackett Publishing, 2011), p. 77.

10. "Discourse," p. 64.

11. "Discourse," p. 73.

12. Biographical details are drawn from Jane Moore, *Mary Wollstonecraft* (Plymouth, UK: Northcote House Publishers, 1999).

13. Philosopher's note: For a more nuanced look at the reception of Wollstonecraft's work, see R. M. James, "On the Reception of Mary Wollstonecraft's *A Vindication of the Rights of Women*," *Journal of the History of Ideas* 39, no. 2 (1978): 293–302.

14. Mary Wollstonecraft, *A Vindication of the Rights of Men and A Vindication of the Rights of Women* (Cambridge: Cambridge University Press, 1995), p. 230.

15. *Rights of Women*, p. 231.

16. *Rights of Women*, p. 234.

17. *Rights of Women*, p. 239.

18. For an in-depth look at this question and Wollstonecraft's ideas about contempt, see Ross Carroll, *Uncivil Mirth: Ridicule in Enlightenment Britain* (Princeton, NJ: Princeton University Press, 2021), especially Chapter Six.

19. *Rights of Men*, p. 5.

20. *Rights of Men*, pp. 6–7.

21. *Rights of Men*, p. 7.

22. *Rights of Men*, p. 8.

23. *Uncivil Mirth*, pp. 197–200.

24. Philosopher's note: These same features of contempt are found in contemporary accounts. This section draws on the following literature: William Ian Miller, *The Anatomy of Disgust* (Cambridge, MA: Harvard University Press, 1997); Michelle Mason, "Contempt as a Moral Attitude," *Ethics* 113, no. 2 (2003): 234–272; and "Contempt: At the Limits of Reactivity," in *The Moral Psychology of Contempt*, ed. Michelle Mason, pp. 173–192 (New York: Rowman & Littlefield, 2018); Macalester Bell, "A Woman's Scorn: Toward a Feminist Defense of Contempt as a Moral Emotion," *Hypatia* 20, no. 4 (2005): 80–93; and *Hard Feelings: The Moral Psychology of Contempt* (New York: Oxford University Press, 2013); Karen Stohr, "Our New Age of Contempt," *The New York Times*, January 23, 2017, https://www.nytimes.com/2017/01/23/opinion/our-new-age-of-contempt.html; Stephen Darwall, "Contempt as an Other-Characterizing 'Hierarchizing' Attitude," in *The Moral Psychology of Contempt*, ed. Michelle Mason, pp. 193–215 (New York: Rowman & Littlefield, 2018); David Sussman, "Above and Beneath Contempt," in *The Moral Psychology of Contempt*, ed. Michelle Mason, pp. 153–172 (New York: Rowman & Littlefield, 2018).

25. Kate Abramson. "A Sentimentalist's Defense of Contempt, Shame, and Disdain," in *The Oxford Handbook of Philosophy of Emotion*, ed. Peter Goldie, pp. 189–213 (Oxford: Oxford University Press, 2009); "Contempt as a Moral Attitude," "At the Limits of Reactivity," "A Woman's Scorn," and *Hard Feelings*.

26. *Hard Feelings*, pp. 200–208.

27. Philosopher's note: My discussion here draws on *Anatomy of Disgust*, especially Chapter 9.

28. "Above and Beneath Contempt," pp. 154–156.

29. *Souls*, p. 10.

30. *Souls*, p. 11.

31. *Souls*, p. 11.

32. W. E. B. Du Bois, *Darkwater: Voices from within the Veil*, ed. Henry Louis Gates Jr. (New York: Oxford University Press, 2007), p. 6.

33. Du Bois, *Darkwater*, p. 6.
34. W. E. B. Du Bois, *Dusk of Dawn*. ed. Henry Louis Gates Jr. (New York: Oxford University Press: 2007), p. 7.
35. "Devil Baby," p. 94.
36. "Devil Baby," p. 100.
37. Jane Addams, *Democracy and Social Ethics* (Chicago: University of Illinois Press, 2002), p. 9.
38. *Democracy*, p. 8.
39. Philosopher's note: I presented portions of this section at the Central Division Meeting of the American Philosophical Association in February 2021 and the Society for the Advancement of American Philosophy's annual meeting in March 2023. The literature on double-consciousness is enormous, but philosophers typically don't explore Du Bois's other work for resources on contempt. My views about Du Bois have been informed by the following literature: Thomas C. Holt, "The Political Uses of Alienation: W. E. B. Du Bois on Politics, Race, and Culture, 1903–1940," *American Quarterly* 42, no. 2 (1990): 301–232; Dickinson D. Bruce Jr., "W. E. B. Du Bois and the Idea of Double Consciousness," *American Literature* 64, no. 2 (1992): 299–309; Paul Gilroy, *The Black Atlantic: Modernity and Double Consciousness* (Cambridge, MA: Harvard University Press, 1993); Ross Posnock, "How It Feels to Be a Problem: Du Bois, Fanon, and the 'Impossible Life' of the Black Intellectual," *Critical Inquiry* 23, no. 2 (1997): 323–349; Ernest Allen Jr., "Du Boisian Double Consciousness: The Unsustainable Argument," *The Massachusetts Review* 43, no. 2 (2002): 217–253; George Yancy, "W. E. B. Du Bois on Whiteness and the Pathology of Black Double Consciousness," *APA Newsletter on Philosophy and the Black Experience* 4, no. 1 (2004): 9–22; Paget Henry, "Africana Phenomenology: Its Philosophical Implications," *CLR James Journal* 11, no.1 (2005): 79–112; Robert Gooding-Williams, *In the Shadow of Du Bois: Afro-Modern Political Thought* (Cambridge, MA: Harvard University Press, 2009); Ryan Schneider, *The Public Intellectualism of Ralph Waldo Emerson and W. E. B. Du Bois: Emotional Dimensions of Race and Reform* (New York: Palgrave Macmillan, 2010); Lawrie Balfour, *Democracy's Reconstruction: Thinking Politically with W. E. B. Du Bois* (New York: Oxford University Press, 2011); Emmanuel C. Eze, "On Double Consciousness," *Callaloo* 34, no. 3 (2011): 877–898; Franklin M. Kirkland, "On Du Bois' Notion of Double Consciousness," *Philosophy Compass* (2013): 137–148; Robert Grotjohn, "'Contempt' in W. E. B. Du Bois' 'Of Our Spiritual Strivings,'" *The Explicator* 70, no. 3 (2012): 213–218; Kwame

Anthony Appiah, *Lines of Descent: W. E. B. Du Bois and the Emergence of Identity* (Cambridge, MA: Harvard University Press, 2014).

40. *Souls*, p. 10.
41. *Souls*, p. 10.
42. W. E. B. Du Bois, *The Autobiography of W. E. B. Du Bois: A Soliloquy on Viewing My Life from the Last Decade of its First Century*, ed. Henry Louis Gates Jr. (New York: Oxford University Press, 2007), p. 86.
43. *Dusk of Dawn*, p. 18.
44. Philosopher's note: Both Watson and Hughey argue that "The Souls of White Folk" is meant to harken to "Of Our Spiritual Strivings." See Veronica Watson, *The Souls of White Folk: African American Writers Theorize Whiteness* (Jackson: University Press of Mississippi, 2013) and Matthew W. Hughey, "'The Souls of White Folk' (1920–2020): A Century of Peril and Prophecy," *Ethnic and Racial Studies* 43, no.8 (2020): 1307–1332.
45. *Darkwater*, p. 15.
46. *Darkwater*, p. 15.
47. *Darkwater*, p. 15.
48. *Darkwater*, p. 15.
49. *Darkwater*, p. 15.
50. *Darkwater*, p. 16.
51. *Darkwater*, p. 16.
52. *Darkwater*, p. 18.
53. *Darkwater*, p. 25.
54. *Dusk of Dawn*, p. 77.
55. *Dusk of Dawn*, p. 77.
56. *Darkwater*, p. 71.

Conclusion

1. *Human, All too Human*, II.2.37, p. 319.
2. The information about Thoreau's life comes from his own telling in *Walden* and other sources. See Henry David Thoreau, *Walden and Other Writings*, ed. Brooks Atkinson (New York: The Modern Library, 2000); Robert A. Gross, "'That Terrible Thoreau': Concord and Its Hermit," in *A Historical Guide to Henry David Thoreau*, ed. William E. Cain, pp. 181–241 (New York: Oxford University Press, 2000); Walter Harding, "Thoreau's Reputation." in *The Cambridge Companion to Henry David Thoreau*, ed. Joel Myerson, pp. 1–11 (New York: Cambridge University Press, 1995).
3. *Walden*, p. 38.

4. *Walden*, p. 19.
5. *Walden*, p. 86.
6. " 'That Terrible Thoreau,'" p. 187.
7. "Thoreau's Reputation," pp. 1–2; " 'That Terrible Thoreau,'" pp. 182–183.
8. " 'That Terrible Thoreau,'" pp. 191–196.
9. *Walden*, p. 35.
10. *Walden*, p. 86.
11. *Walden*, p. 83.
12. *Walden*, p. 83.
13. *Walden*, p. 178.
14. *Walden*, p. 82.
15. *Walden*, pp. 91–92.
16. *Walden*, p. 198.
17. *Walden*, p. 206. Philosopher's note: Thoreau's views on the "animal within" are complex in this part of *Walden*. I think he ultimately embraces it, but that's an argument I don't offer here. For one version of reconciling these passages, see Jim Cheney, "The Dusty World: Wildness and Higher Laws in Thoreau's *Walden*," *Ethics and the Environment* 1 (1996): 75–90.
18. Philosopher's note: Wolf attributes this view to Bernard Williams. I think she's right about this. See "Meaning and Morality," in *The Variety of Values*, p. 131.
19. *Hacking Life*, pp. 13–14.

Index

For the benefit of digital users, indexed terms that span two pages (e.g., 52–53) may, on occasion, appear on only one of those pages.